On You[illegible]

Lincolnshire

Roger Fox

COUNTRYSIDE BOOKS
NEWBURY, BERKSHIRE

First published 2002

COUNTRYSIDE BOOKS
3 Catherine Road
Newbury, Berkshire

To view our complete range of books,
please visit us at
www.countrysidebooks.co.uk

ISBN 1 85306 731 8

Cover picture supplied by
Cyclographic Publications

Designed by Graham Whiteman

Produced through MRM Associates Ltd., Reading
Printed in Italy

CONTENTS

AREA MAP SHOWING THE LOCATIONS OF THE RIDES

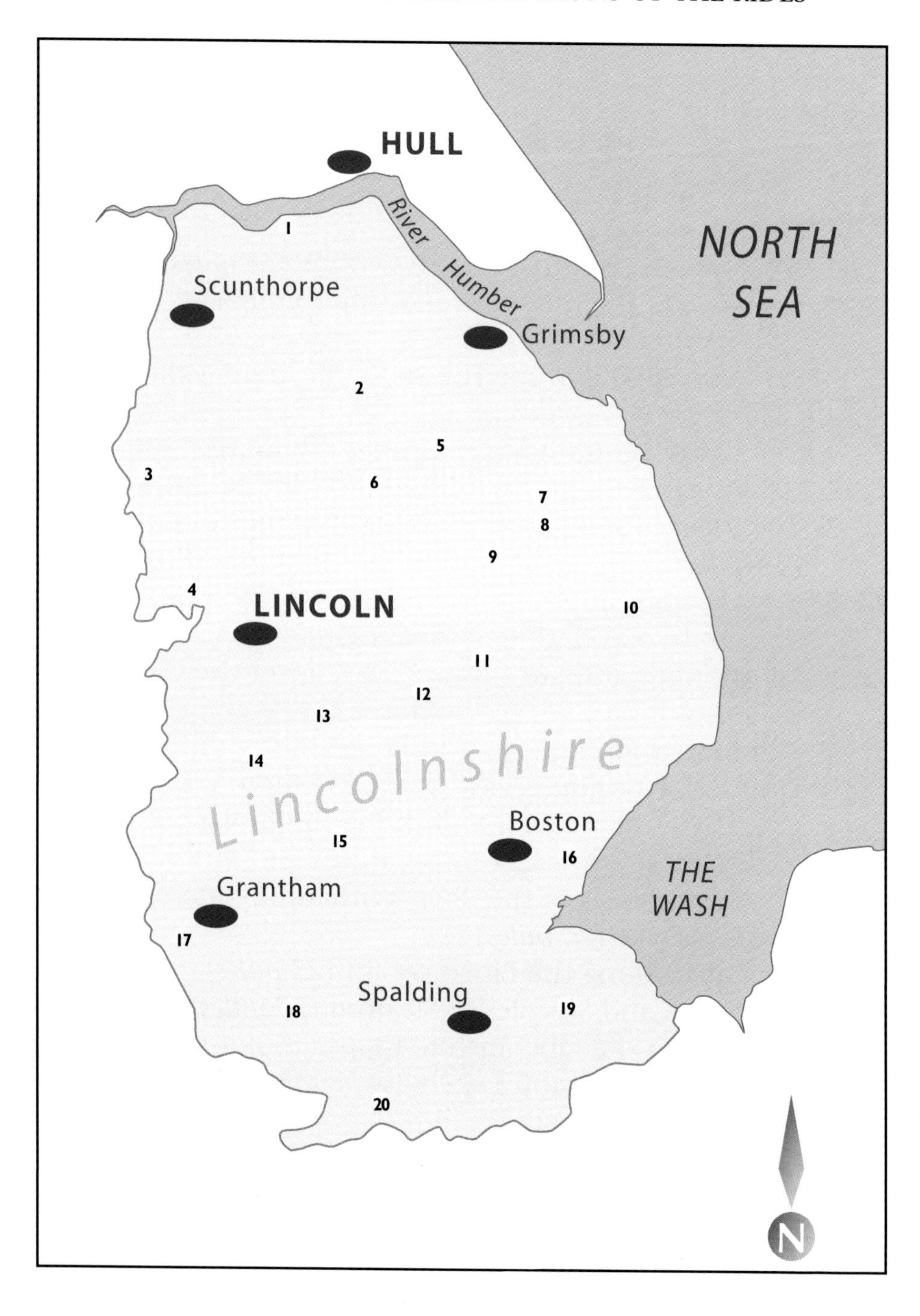

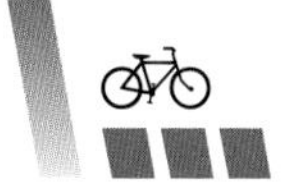

INTRODUCTION

Walking is often prescribed as the best way to view the English countryside. But only so many miles may be covered on foot in one day. Motor transport, on the other hand, can convey you vast distances at high speed – but everything flashes past before you have time to look, and as much again is missed altogether. No, the ideal mode of transport must enable you to examine your discoveries at leisure, while placing little limitation on the extent of your journey. Cycling, of course, is the answer.

The only missing piece of this puzzle is where to enjoy this healthy and absurdly inexpensive method of moving freely around the landscape under your own steam. An area which is relatively quiet and unspoilt is what is required, with lots of suitable rural lanes. Perhaps a wide variety of terrains to choose from – vast arable fenlands, rolling hills, lofty chalk escarpments looking down to broad wooded river valleys and coastal plains. Hidden churches in countless sleepy villages, steeples rising behind ancient market squares, and an historic city dominated by one of Europe's most spectacular medieval cathedrals. Welcome to Lincolnshire.

The routes in this book have been selected to reflect the enormous diversity of the Lincolnshire landscape, and each is loosely centred around a theme. I have personally ridden all twenty routes taking note of signposting, road names and visible features likely to ensure that you won't get lost. It is a good idea to read right through a route before setting out so that you note any places where you want to spend more time, and to avoid regretting what you have missed!

The rides vary in length from 15 to 32 miles, and most should be considered a full day's outing – especially if you are to find time to investigate all the nooks and crannies. Main roads have been avoided where possible and you will spend most of your time on charming country roads linking villages and towns, each waiting to share its individual story with you. So whether you prefer to ride alone or you are planning a day with friends or family, get on your bike and come and discover the secrets of Lincolnshire.

Roger Fox

GUIDE TO USING THIS BOOK

Each route is preceded by information to help you:

The **number of miles** is the total for the ride. All of the routes, however, can be abbreviated or expanded with the aid of your Ordnance Survey maps.

The **introduction** gives the broad picture of the route and the reason for its inclusion. The types of road surface, gradient and terrain are also mentioned here, as are particular features seen along the way.

The **starting point** provides details of how to reach the start of the ride and of suitable car parking nearby.

Places for refreshment are also included, sometimes tearooms or inns serving good food, and there are others just waiting for you to discover them. Don't forget – it is against the law to ride under the influence of drink or drugs.

THE ROUTES

Each route is accompanied by a **sketch map**. These maps are intended to give you a general idea of the route, but are not detailed enough to be route guides. It is strongly recommended that you also carry the relevant Ordnance Survey map for the area and use it in conjunction with the sketch maps.

At the end of each chapter you will find brief details of **places of interest** along the ride. These include notes about architecture, history, legends and people connected with the entry.

SAFETY

Common sense and a sound knowledge of the Highway Code are essential requirements when considering a bike ride. Some forethought and planning are also advisable, so that you are in a good position to cope with any problems that occur. Before you set off check that your machine is in a roadworthy condition, paying particular attention to brakes and tyres. In the event of roadside repairs becoming necessary your toolkit should be supplemented by a pump, tyre levers, a spare inner tube and the knowledge of how to use them. In addition do not set off without clothing which is both waterproof and warm, a snack, a drink and some money. In the unlikely occurrence of an emergency you might also be thankful for a mobile phone.

As far as clothing is concerned a well-fitting helmet, though not compulsory, is certainly advisable. But most important is an item of brightly coloured clothing or reflective material, especially in poor lighting conditions. Remember it is the responsibility of the cyclist to ensure that he or she is visible to other road users.

1

Barton-upon-Humber and the Wolds

27 miles

As well as being a thriving market town, Barton-upon-Humber is also the start of the Viking Way long distance footpath and the best place from which to view the world's longest single span suspension bridge. From Barton this route traces the edge of the Wolds, giving excellent views westwards over the Ancholme valley, before crossing the Wolds and returning through once prosperous villages near the coast – and almost all on good tarmac surfaces. Fine examples of typical Lincolnshire brick architecture are to be found in each town and village, the only stone buildings being imposing parish churches and the highlight of this expedition, the ruins of the once powerful Thornton Abbey.

Maps: OS Landranger 112 Scunthorpe & Gainsborough and 113 Grimsby (GR 027234).

Starting point: The Humber Bridge Viewing Area at the north end of Waterside Road in Barton-upon-Humber – there is a large free car park here. The town of Barton is easily located just off the A15. There is also a good train service to Barton from Grimsby.

Refreshments: You will find a comprehensive selection of restaurants, inns and shops in Barton, while Goxhill and Barrow are also well catered for. Otherwise inns serving food will be found in most of the villages en route, with Elsham being the notable exception. But possibly the highest recommendation is reserved for the picnic site overlooking the dramatic gatehouse at Thornton Abbey.

Before setting off it is worth exploring the area around the Humber Bridge Viewing Area. The brick 'lookout' on the seawall was built in 1880 as a coastguard station, and is now the official starting point for the Viking Way, a long distance path established in 1976 stretching 147 miles to Oakham on the shores of Rutland Water. The coastal path enables you to study the bridge at close quarters, while the nearby disused clay pits have been converted into an attractive stretch of ponds, woods and walkways.

From the car park head south along Waterside Road and **turn R** into Far Ings Road at the Sloop Inn. The forbidding shadow of the Humber Bridge passes overhead (note that this is the access point onto it for those who intend to include an exhilarating trip across the River Humber and back), and in ¾ mile you **turn L** at a crossroads (simply signed 'All Routes') to ascend the hill as far as the main A1077. **Turn R** (signed 'Scunthorpe') and continue with due care, contrasting the serene view over Read's Island and the Humber with the stern outline of the distant cement plant. After 2 miles you swoop down a long steep hill into South Ferriby, where you **turn L** off the main road onto the B1204 (signed 'Brigg'). This road will guide you between the steep Wolds scarp and the broad Ancholme valley for the next 6 miles, through a string of interesting villages, each boasting a delightful church and groups of neat brick buildings. The first of these is Horkstow, where in 1796 a substantial section of a Roman mosaic pavement was discovered, portraying scenes of a chariot race and Orpheus taming the wild beasts. The next village is Saxby All Saints – both Horkstow and Saxby boast interesting bridges over the new River Ancholme, reached by lanes leading across the carrs, the once marshy lowlands beside the river. Sadly no route links the two bridges, and they must be treated as separate excursions.

Bonby, whose red brick church tower capped by a tiled pyramid roof looks somewhat Tuscan, is followed by Worlaby, slightly haughtier than the preceding villages. As you explore the village look for the handsome Victorian stone drinking fountain, fed continuously by a nearby spring.

The B1204 ends abruptly near the entrance to Elsham Hall Country and Wildlife Park – **turn L** (signed 'Elsham') onto the B1206 and, following the edge of the woods, **turn R** (signed 'Elsham') to enter the village of Elsham. At the crossroads in the village centre **turn L** (unsigned) into Front Street, then immediately **turn L** again into Maltkiln Lane, which arcs up the hill towards All Saints' church, hidden in the trees which cover the whole of the hillside. On either side of the medieval church doorway is a worn stone panel carved in the 13th century, depicting details from the Last Judgement, including a figure rising from a coffin. Beyond the church **turn L** to rejoin Front Street and climb through the woods to a disused hilltop quarry. **Turn L** here and, at a five-way junction, **turn R** (signed 'Wootton') to pass a tall communications pylon on your left.

You now leave behind the views over the Ancholme plain to cross the chalky plateau of the Lincolnshire Wolds. Remain on this road and in 3½ miles you arrive at a junction where, straight ahead, you spot the village sign for Wootton. Along the High Street and into the heart of the village a wonderful rural scene is unveiled. Willow trees surround a large open pond covered in lily pads, and behind the houses fronting the pond rises the ancient weathered ironstone tower of Saint Andrew's church.

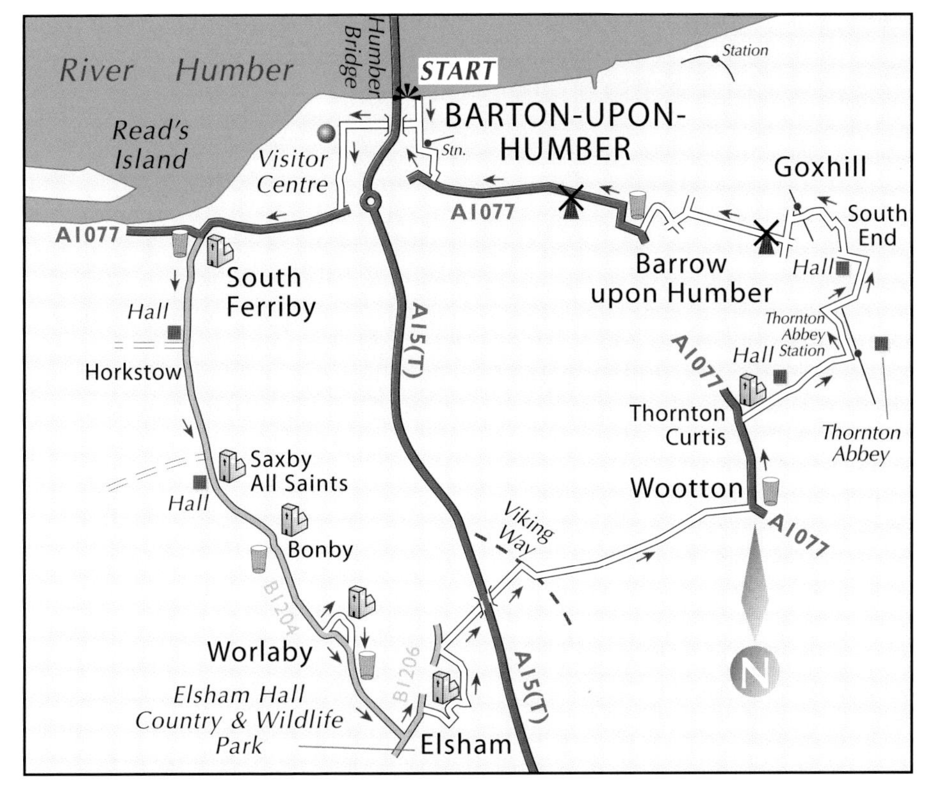

Just beyond this setting is the village inn, the Nag's Head, at which you **turn L** onto the A1077 (signed Barton).

A mile later you reach the small village of Thornton Curtis and another Saint Andrew's church, this one the proud guardian of a rare and remarkable square font carved from black Tournai marble. However, just before the village, you **turn R** into Station Road (signed 'East Halton'). Eventually you come to a railway line, but instead of following the road left, continue through a white gate and over the tracks. Another gate leads you onto a wide grassy lane with the glorious gatehouse of Thornton Abbey now in full view. Upon reaching the remains of the abbey you will find them free to visit and open at most times – a thorough inspection should not be omitted.

Leaving the abbey return to the railway on a road parallel to the grass track and, ½ mile past the level crossing, **turn R** into Soft Lane (signed 'Goxhill South End'). At the next T-junction **turn L** into South End and look carefully to spy the lofty medieval manor known wrongly as Goxhill Priory, masked by a range of farm buildings on your left. Now **turn R** into Thorn Lane, which weaves its way into the centre of Goxhill, where you **turn L** into Howe Lane.

Goxhill is a sizeable village whose erstwhile importance is reflected by an enormous stately church tower and a maze of narrow streets flanked by imposing houses. Cross the railway once more and continue to the next junction at which you **turn L** into Thornton Road. At the crossroads **turn R** (signed 'Barrow') and, in another mile, **turn L** onto the B1206 (signed 'Brigg'), then **turn R** onto the B1402 (signed 'Barton') to enter Barrow-upon-Humber.

Having passed the old wooden village pump, look for a road to your left, untitled but leading you clearly to the impressive tower of Holy Trinity church. Keeping the church to your right you now curve left into Barrow High Street, a showcase of fine buildings from many periods and a surprising find in such a village. Like Goxhill, Barrow was obviously a place of some importance. Remains of an ancient monastery and a Saxon castle have been identified here but it was chiefly as the town adjacent to the nearby port or 'haven' that Barrow prospered. Passing the small market square and the stump of an old butter cross, **turn R** into Barton Lane (signed 'A1077 Barton'), **turn R** again at the top of the hill into Ferry Road, and finally **turn L** (signed A1077 Barton) at a mini-roundabout.

Follow this road for 2 miles, taking advantage of the cycle lane and pausing at a picnic site to enjoy the superb view over the Humber. From New Holland pier to the east and along the shore, your gaze will lead across the mighty Humber Bridge to the Hessle foreshore and over the whole of the city of Kingston-upon-Hull. Eventually you reach the small market place in Barton-upon-Humber with, hopefully, time to explore this fascinating little town. If you **turn R** into George Street, **turn L** into the High Street, **turn R** again into Queen Street, then **turn L** again into Butts Road you will find yourself at the southern end of Waterside Road, with the bridge viewing area car park now just ½ mile away.

THE HUMBER BRIDGE

Opened in 1981, the statistics surrounding this elegant structure are mind-boggling. The two piers reach a height of 510 ft, and the distance between them is over 1,500 yards. At a total weight exceeding half a million tons, the bridge took 9 years to construct. Now compare this to the two charming bridges at Horkstow and Saxby, both built in the 1840s to serve the brick kilns along the Ancholme, and both neatly painted in red and green. Horkstow, Sir John Rennie's only design of this type, is one of the earliest suspension bridges, while Saxby is a single span framework made from wrought iron.

2

Caistor and the Estates of Lord Yarborough

17 miles

This ride takes you from the former market town of Caistor on a tour of the sumptuous environs of Brocklesby Hall, the neat estate villages which surround it, and several other impressive architectural monuments which also owe their existence to the Earls of Yarborough. It is an ideal ride to choose for the winter months when these landmarks become more clear through the naked trees, and you remain on excellent road surfaces throughout. Be sure to leave yourself enough time to explore Caistor itself.

Maps: OS Landranger 113 Grimsby and 112 Scunthorpe & Gainsborough (GR 118013).

Starting point: The market square in Caistor, where you will find ample car parking. Caistor is easily located just off the A46 between Market Rasen and Grimsby.

Refreshments: Caistor offers only a couple of public houses, but has numerous shops. Around the route, as well as the New Inn at Great Limber and the Cross Keys at Grasby, there is an inn at Kirmington and small village shops in Great Limber and Brocklesby.

At the top of Caistor's small market square a narrow lane leads left from the Cornhouse Cellars to join the old High Street. **Turn R** onto this and climb steeply out of the town. Notice a curious round turret and castellated wall at the entrance to Mill Lane. At the top of the hill is an inn called the Fleece. **Turn L** here onto the A1173 (signed 'Immingham') and in ½ a mile **turn L** onto a minor road (signed 'Great Limber').

Above the trees ahead of you looms a colossal monument, a tapering square column, 128 feet high and capped by an elegant lantern. This is Pelham's Pillar, raised in 1849 to celebrate the achievement of Charles Anderson Pelham, the first Lord Yarborough, of planting 12,500,000 trees in these woods between 1787 and 1828. An equally arresting building is set in a clearing at the foot of the tower, a lodge with a rustic veranda and Gothic windows. When clouds of smoke curl from the chimneys this could be the entrance to an enchanted forest, and the chalet might even be

Brocklesby Hall

made of gingerbread! Rather less romantic is the next scene to appear on the horizon, the grim outlines of the industrial plants along the Humber Bank. However the view soon improves as you proceed unerringly along this road for 3 miles through alternate woods and rolling fields. Of particular interest is the bright green dome of a mausoleum in the distance, and it is towards this that you **turn L** at the foot of a dip (signed 'Great Limber') into Brickyard.

Passing the site of a medieval manor based around a small monastery on your right you come across a wonderful setting, a large pond fringed by lily pads, bulrushes and drooping willows, with the delights surrounding it reflected on its surface. Among these are the ironstone tower of Saint Peter's church, while behind you the large thatched house, whose white stone walls reach a thickness of 7 ft, is the 17th century Priest's House. Continue in your original direction along Church Lane to a major junction in the centre of Great Limber. Here to your left is an old-fashioned village shop, to your right the excellent New Inn (selling Sargent's local ice-cream!), and ahead of you the railings and deep woods guarding the Pelham Mausoleum. Exercising due care **turn R** onto the main A18.

By now you will have noted that most of the houses look distinctly

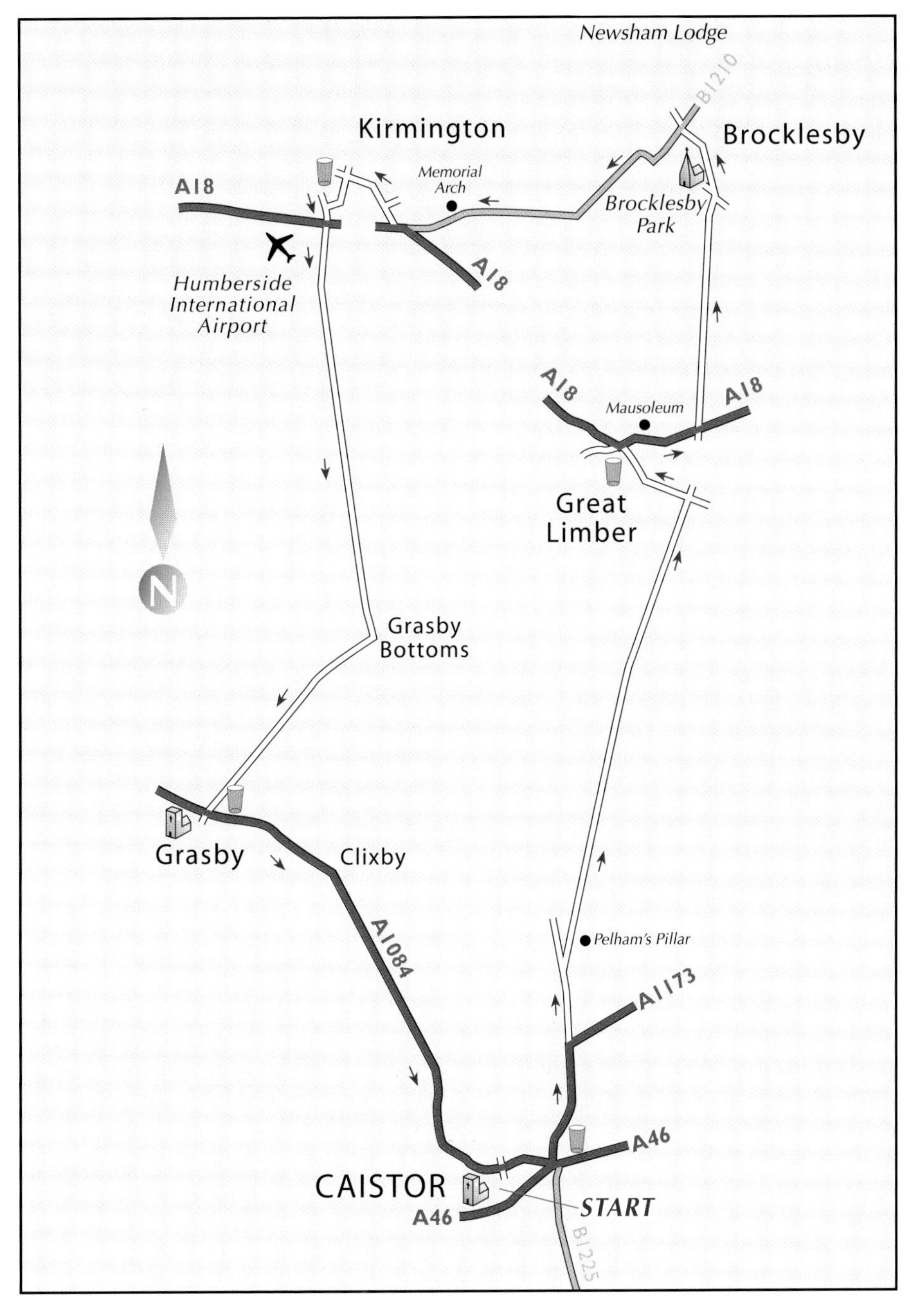
Newsham Lodge
B1210
Kirmington
Brocklesby
A18
Memorial Arch
Brocklesby Park
Humberside International Airport
A18
A18
A18
Mausoleum
Great Limber
N
Grasby Bottoms
Grasby
Clixby
A1084
Pelham's Pillar
A1173
A46
CAISTOR
START
A46
B1225

similar, with the same style of wooden fascia capped by a pointed finial – you have entered the Brocklesby estate, the lands of Lord Yarborough. Some of these houses even bear the family crest, and the general air of affluence is emphasised by a selection of tall chimneys of every type and design. Passing a charming old corner barn on your right with its unique open lattice brickwork, continue until you reach the village's last cottage and **turn L** (signed 'Brocklesby').

After a mile of ever more opulent countryside you pass the Brocklesby Hunt kennels on your left to arrive at a T-junction next to Whip's Lodge. Take the narrow road to your left through the huge white gates and enter the grounds of Brocklesby Hall. As you are ushered between high-walled gardens and past a succession of elegant lodges you will feel privileged to be enjoying such magnificence. The road curves and you may catch a glimpse of the Hall itself through the woods to your right. In fact good views of the Hall are elusive – Capability Brown certainly did his job well here. Stop to admire the rustic church tower and its fine lead spire, then retrace your tracks to Whip's Lodge, as the road beyond the church is private.

At the lodge **turn L** onto the B1211 (signed 'Ulceby') and, having enjoyed another display of fine estate cottages through Brocklesby village, **turn L** at the major crossroads (signed 'Kirmington'). This road descends to a bridge over the lake before twisting between ranges of imposing stables and farm buildings adjacent to the Hall. Leaving the grounds through twin stone gate pillars the quality of the view continues for the next mile. In the distance to your right spot Newsham Lodge, a castle-style folly, while on your left, beyond railed horse paddocks and a cricket pitch overlooked by a tiny overgrown pavilion, the woods lead away from Brocklesby Hall to the mausoleum at Great Limber.

As you re-enter the woods you will be astonished by the spectacle of the stone Memorial Arch, spanning the road in front of you. This is an extraordinary structure to come across in the English countryside. Through the arch you arrive back at the busy A18. You might prefer to dismount here, **turn R** and walk the few yards to the next side road, into which you also **turn R** (signed 'Kirmington'). The ancient weathered tower of Saint Helen's in Kirmington also boasts a fine spire, rare in this part of Lincolnshire, and made of copper. **Turn L** at a small crossroads into Post Office Lane and, at the junction with East End, **turn R** to head out of the village. At the next T-junction **turn L**, cross the A18 with care and continue straight ahead as the huge arch disappears behind you, and the cultivated woods and pastures of Yarborough give way to a more open landscape.

Humberside Airport now occupies the land to your right and you climb this road to plummet 3 miles later into the wooded valley of Grasby Bottoms. On the way espy a hidden summerhouse, built in a classical style, with a pediment filled by a curious fanned circle of wooden logs. **Turn R** at the crossroads (signed 'Grasby') and again climb until you meet another main road at the Cross Keys inn, high above the village of Grasby. From here the panorama extends from Pelham's Pillar to Caistor, along the high scarp of the Wolds, and across the vale below to the cathedral at Lincoln. **Turn L** at this junction onto the A1084 (signed 'Caistor'), and descend to the tiny hamlet of Clixby. All Hallows on your left now calls itself no more than a 'wayside shrine'. It was once much larger but Clixby never recovered from the Black Death, and today the only inhabitants of this place are pigs – field after field of them!

Two miles later Caistor welcomes you once more. Opposite the imposing Holly House **turn R** into Chapel Street to pass a series of fascinating old buildings, which continue around the corner into Church Street, where the 17th century stone Grammar School is situated. Dismount and walk along the charming Church Folly, below the enormous tower of the church to emerge at the Syfer Spring, feeding a small brick-lined corner pool. From here Fountain Street leads you back towards the market square.

CAISTOR

Caistor was established by the Romans as a walled town in the 4th century – look in the churchyard for a fragment of these walls. In the church itself, mounted in a glass case, is the 'Gad Whip', ritually cracked over the vicar's head each Palm Sunday. Elsewhere there are hidden delights around every corner of Caistor, and the Caistor Society have been good enough to erect a series of blue plaques, explaining important sites and dates.

BROCKLESBY HALL

Beautifully set amid lily ponds and rebuilt in 1710 from red brick with stone dressing, the family seat of the Earls of Yarborough is a storehouse of art treasures. The extensive grounds were laid out by Lancelot 'Capability' Brown, and although the tradition of sympathetic forest management has continued to this day, it is as home to the controversial Brocklesby Hunt that the Hall is now more well known.

The park is entered from the west via the massive Memorial Arch erected in 1865. The badly eroded plinths and pillars lead up to an inscription: 'To Charles Anderson Worsley, 2nd Earl of Yarborough, by his tenants and friends'.

At the south end of the park, actually in the next village of Great Limber, is a smaller but more accomplished memorial – the Pelham Mausoleum designed by James Wyatt in 1794, and considered to be his finest work. Built in memory of Sophia Aufrere, the wife of Charles Pelham, who died at the early age of 33, the circular mausoleum has a copper domed roof, and contains a central statue of Sophia carved in marble.

3

Gainsborough and the Forests of the Trent Valley

26 miles

Your route is centred upon Gainsborough, whose industrial heritage of engineering, brewing and rope-making gives way to a series of charming rural villages, ancient church towers and a trek along an exciting forest track. You then head towards the River Trent, the inspiration for a literary classic, and finish at a splendid medieval masterpiece – with hopefully time to investigate this and the other attractions in Gainsborough.

Map: OS Landranger 112 Scunthorpe & Gainsborough (GR 813900).

Starting point: The Old Hall in Gainsborough. From the traffic lights at the bridge over the Trent head north along Bridge Street, which successively becomes Caskgate and Ropery Road. Half a mile along here turn right into Gladstone Street and the Hall is on your right. There is parking in the streets around the Hall.

Refreshments: You will find the expected range of refreshment facilities in Gainsborough. Elsewhere there are good inns serving food in the villages of Corringham, Scotton, Laughton and Morton. The well-prepared might opt for a picnic at one of several woodland sites.

Turn L in front of Gainsborough's Old Hall along Gladstone Street, and then **turn L** again into Ropery Road, later to become Caskgate then Bridge Street. At the traffic lights inspect the forlorn white toll lodges, former guardians of the handsome bridge over the River Trent, toll-free since 1932, before continuing straight ahead into Lea Road. Just before the old Lea Road station building on your right, **turn L** into Foxby Hill and climb through the woods – pause to observe a small memorial to the right commemorating the Battle of Gainsborough in 1643, when Cromwell's troops defeated Charles I's Royalist army on these slopes. At a supermarket a mile later **turn R** (signed 'Upton') to exchange Gainsborough's urban bustle for quiet lanes, woods and open fields.

In 2½ miles this lane passes the perfectly restored Hewitt's Windmill – maybe you will find the doors open and the sails turning. Around a sharp bend, **turn L** into a side lane (signed to

The Old Hall, Gainsborough

'Springthorpe'), and **turn L** again (also signed to 'Springthorpe') opposite the square Anglo-Saxon tower of Heapham's lonely church. Continue through the peaceful hamlet of Springthorpe to the busy A631. With care, **turn L** (signed 'Gainsborough') and then **turn R** (signed 'Aisby') into the village of Corringham. In a setting of neat lawns and cheerful white cottages the notable Saxon church tower, rising behind the most ornate carved stone lychgate, now draws you forward. Follow Middle Street right into East Lane and, passing the last house on your right, **turn L** into an unsigned lane.

Turn L at the next junction (the only sign is for a cycle route in the opposite direction!), divert briefly around a looping lane through a farming hamlet called Aisby, before continuing to a crossroads at which you **turn R** (signed 'Pilham'). **Turn R** again (signed 'Pilham') below Pilham's odd little obelisk of a church tower and proceed as far as an unsigned T-junction. **Turn L** here and pass a sign declaring 'Level crossing closed 10pm to 6am' – I have not tested this but will assume that if you are still cycling hereabouts between these times this is the least of your problems.

Beyond the level crossing **turn R** (signed 'B1205 Kirton Lindsey'). A mile later **turn L** (signed 'Northorpe') and enter the village

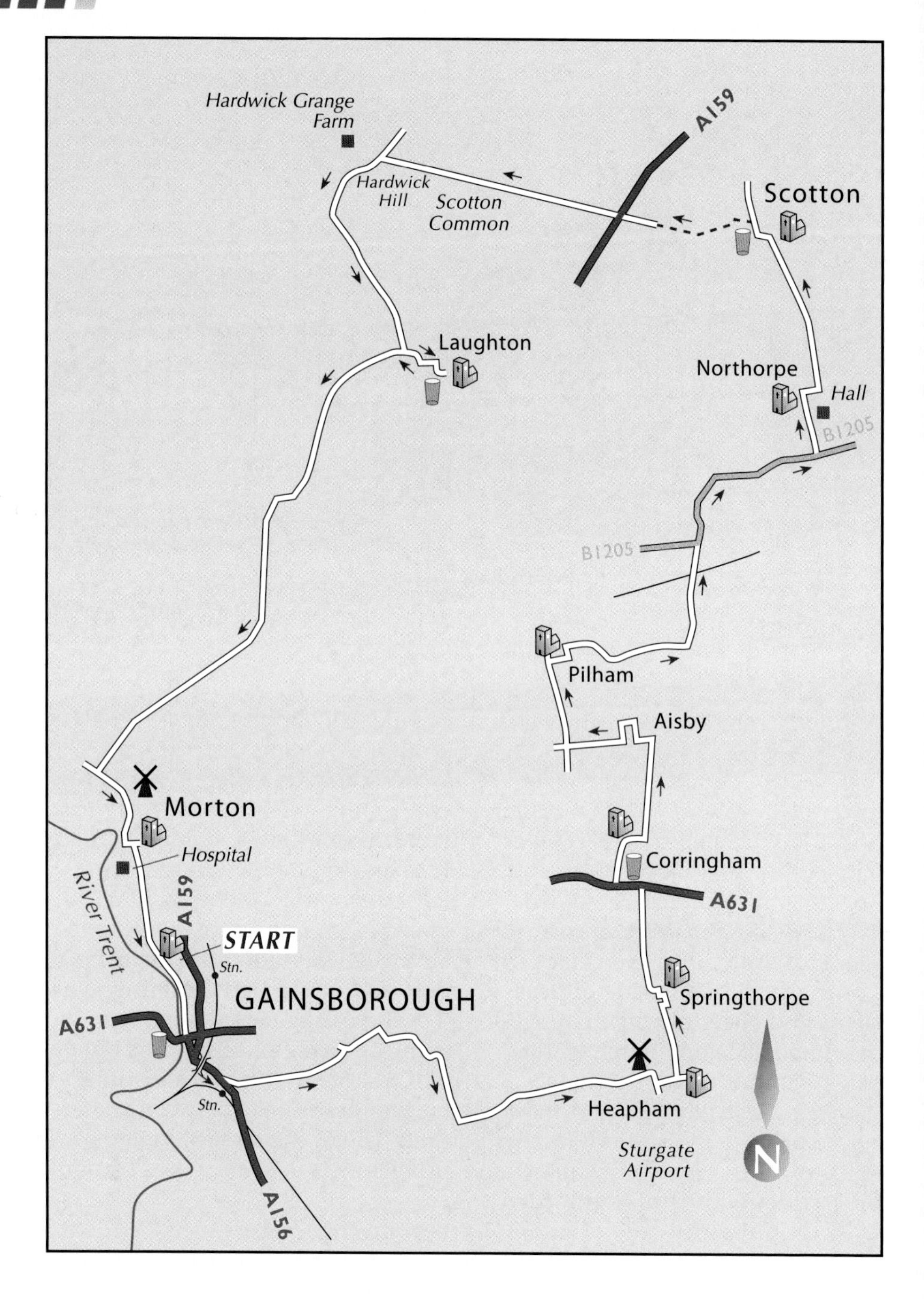
Hardwick Grange
Farm
A159
Hardwick
Hill
Scotton
Common
Scotton
Laughton
Northorpe
Hall
B1205
B1205
Pilham
Aisby
Morton
Hospital
River Trent
A159
START
Stn.
GAINSBOROUGH
A631
Corringham
A631
Springthorpe
Stn.
Heapham
Sturgate
Airport
N
A156

of that name, passing the park containing the ruins of the 16th century Northorpe Hall on your right. The road dips and rises, passes Northorpe's handsome stone church and vicarage, then follows a long open lane into Scotton. In the ivy-clad stone archway opposite the church spot a pair of ancient carved figures, and then **turn L** into Eastgate. Descend until almost out of the village and carefully locate a footpath on your left displaying a 'cycle trail' sign. **Turn L** onto this delightful track which narrows after a while, but which is a privileged way to travel through these woodlands. After a mile the track improves briefly to a metalled surface before emerging at Rainford's Corner on the busy A159. Cross carefully and continue relentlessly ahead for another 2 miles, until this joyride terminates at Hardwick Grange Farm, close to the pine-clad slopes of Hardwick Hill.

Turn L and progress through these enchanting woodland surroundings until you reach the pleasant village of Laughton, and another lofty church tower at the head of an interesting cluster of old village buildings. Back into the woods, return as far as a junction just outside the village, at which you **turn L** (signed 'Wildsworth'). Now simply follow this road for the next 4 miles, the first 2 miles still sheltered by these vast woodlands, the remainder through more open countryside.

Eventually reaching a junction, **turn L** into Walkerith Road (signed 'Morton') to enter the busy village of Morton, blessed with a number of fine Georgian halls. You can opt to **turn R** at Eliot House on your right to enjoy a brief section of the Trent river bank alongside the disused wharf buildings, before re-emerging on your original route at the Crooked Billet. Morton is contiguous with Gainsborough, and you **turn R** opposite a public house named the Ship into Ropery Road once more. Having passed the impressive John Coupland Hospital on your right, proud ranks of terraced houses now lead you back towards Gladstone Street on your left, and the Old Hall.

GAINSBOROUGH OLD HALL

This magnificent 15th century manor house is one of the country's best preserved. Behind the black and white timber-framed Great Hall rise tall brick-built towers and chimneys, housing a superb medieval kitchen – Richard III and Henry VIII number among the guests who banqueted here.

LAUGHTON FOREST

Although it was planted mainly with conifers in the late 18th century, your trek through this forest passes by rare heathland areas and peaty pools, where distinctive wetland flora flourish among the birch trees. Look for woodpeckers and heron as well as roe deer and squirrels. To the south Owlet Plantation is mainly oak and birch, and supports rare species of butterfly and damselfly.

4

The Fossdyke: Cathedrals, Castles and Canals

26 miles

For almost 2,000 years the Fossdyke has linked the mighty River Trent with the rivers of eastern England, and this outing focuses on these two important watercourses. The terrain is undulating rather than hilly, and you remain on firm road surfaces throughout. Your route visits a string of villages full of interesting items, the minster at Stow being one of Lincolnshire's must-see treasures.

Map: OS Landranger 121 Lincoln & Newark-on-Trent (GR 897752).

Starting point: Bridge Street in Saxilby, 6 miles west of Lincoln on the A57. Turn off the A57 onto the B1241 (signed 'Saxilby') then immediately left into Bridge Street. Roadside parking can be found in Bridge Street or the adjacent streets. Trains running between Lincoln and Gainsborough also stop in Saxilby.

Refreshments: As well as a couple of public houses in Saxilby there are other good inns in Sturton, Willingham and Torksey, and of course the Cross Keys in Stow and the White Swan at Torksey Lock, mentioned in the route directions.

Set off west along Bridge Street, and follow the curving road all the way round to Saint Botolph's church, Saxilby's oldest building, dating back to Norman times and featuring a seven-arched oak chancel screen from the 15th century. **Turn L** at the junction onto Sturton Road, which leads you to a minor crossroads at which you **turn R** (signed 'Bransby'). The lane you are on passes through Bransby, where you will find the Home of Rest for Horses, a sanctuary caring for 200 animals.

At the main A1500 **turn L** (signed 'Sturton'), immediately **turn R** (signed 'Thorpe-le-Fallows'), then **turn L** again (signed 'Sturton') into Fleets Road, an attractive lane leading into Sturton-by-Stow. At the next T-junction the two inns in the centre of the village lie to your left, but you should **turn R** and prepare yourself for what lies ahead. Soon the startling outline of a colossal Norman minster looms into view here in the depths of the Lincolnshire countryside – this is Stow, the mother of Lincoln Cathedral, herself visible on the skyline to the south. Set alongside the massive walls of the minster,

The Fossdyke in Saxilby

you will find the original village whipping-iron and the excellent Cross Keys, not so much a public house serving food, more a restaurant serving beer.

Leave Stow from the crossroads in the direction marked 'Coates church', your next destination. After 1½ miles **turn L** at another sign for this church, St Edith's, a tiny remote shrine hidden in trees opposite a farmyard at the end of a row of poplars. The contrast with Stow's magnificence is absolute, but the building has a special atmosphere and numbers Lincolnshire's only surviving rood screen and loft among its treasures.

Now retrace your tyre-tracks to the crossroads in Stow, and this time **turn R** (signed 'Willingham-by-Stow'), to continue to the village of that name. Reaching the junction with the High Street, **turn L** (signed 'Kexby') round the spruce tower of Saint Helen's and head towards Kexby, ½ a mile to the north. Do not enter Kexby, rather follow the road left into Kexby Lane, to travel the length of this lane to Knaith Park. Opposite the Stag's Head public house **turn L** into Station Road, cross the railway bridge and descend Knaith Hill to the hamlet of Knaith itself, where you **turn L** (signed 'Lincoln') onto the busy A156. Immediately to

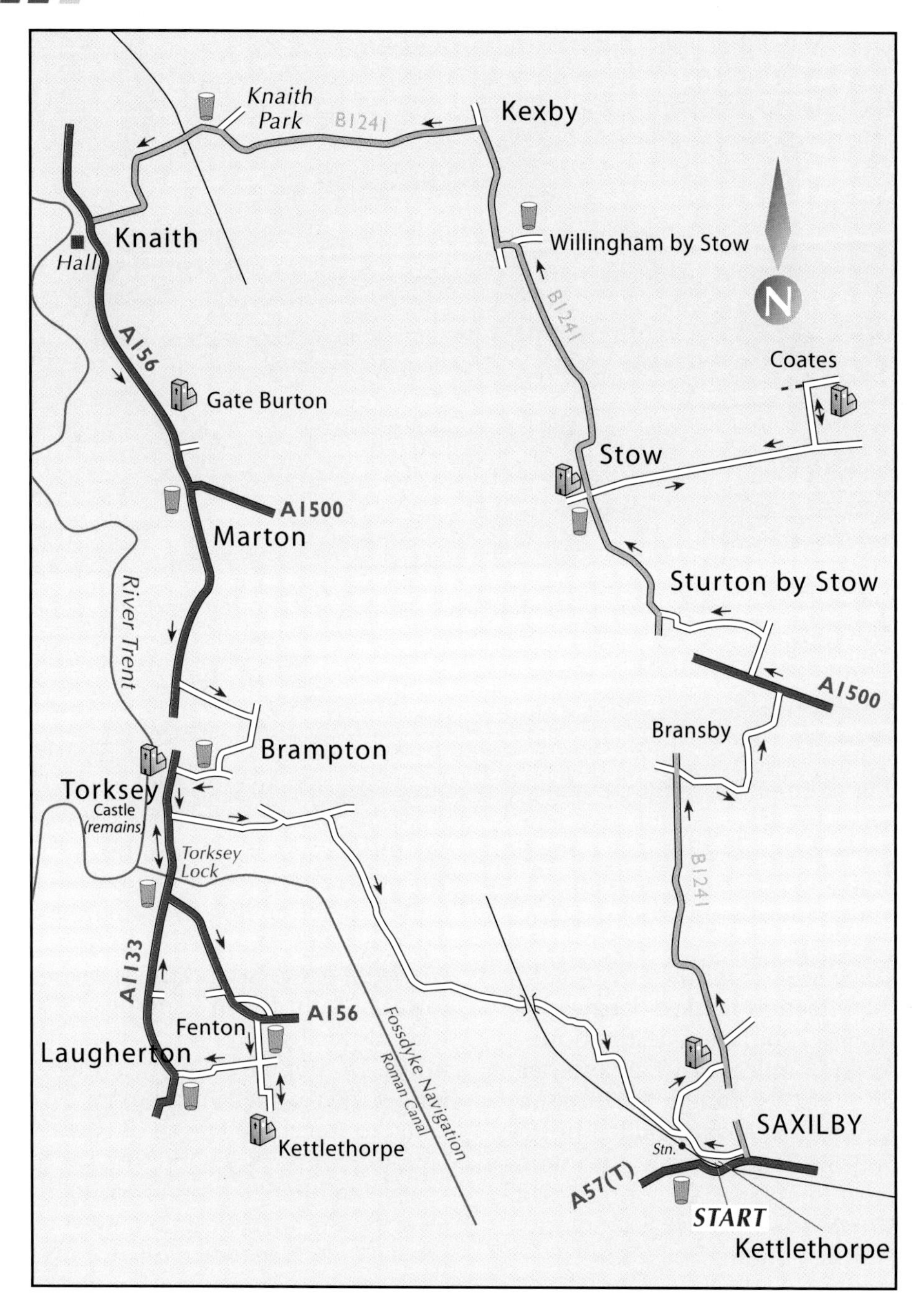
Knaith
Park
B1241
Kexby
Knaith
Hall
Willingham by Stow
B1241
N
A156
Gate Burton
Coates
Stow
A1500
Marton
Sturton by Stow
River Trent
A1500
Bransby
Brampton
Torksey
Castle
(remains)
Torksey
Lock
B1241
A1133
A156
Fenton
Laugherton
Fossdyke Navigation
Roman Canal
SAXILBY
Stn.
Kettlethorpe
A57(T)
START
Kettlethorpe

your right a short track enables you to inspect the peculiar twin naves of Saint Mary's and the curious black and white timbering of Knaith Hall, as well as sneaking a fine view along a wide stretch of the adjacent River Trent.

Continue in your original direction along the main road until the surroundings upgrade to a parkscape, and below a coronet of trees to your right identify a small but perfectly formed temple, known as the 'Shatoo', an outlier of Gate Burton Hall on the other side of the road. The next village of Marton is of considerable historical importance, as it straddles the old Roman Tillbridge Lane, leading west to a nearby ford across the Trent to Segelocum (now Littleborough). Caution must have been required since the Aegir, the formidable tidal bore, comes up the Trent as far as Marton. In the centre of the village is a church (dedicated unusually to Saint Margaret of Antioch), whose tower consists entirely of splendid Saxon herring-bone masonry.

A mile past Marton **turn L** (signed 'Brampton') to divert along a winding lane through the Georgian settlement of Brampton and between golf links on either side. **Turn R** at an unsigned junction beyond which the road returns you to the Trentside highway at the ruined brick piers of Torksey railway viaduct – **turn L** (signed 'Torksey'). Through Torksey locate a padlocked gate on your right opposite the post office. Here, through the trees, is the only view you will gain of the skeletal ruins of Torksey Castle. Built in Elizabethan times to a style and proportion similar to nearby Doddington Hall, this grand mansion was ransacked by the Parliamentarians less than 100 years later and never rebuilt.

A mile further on Torksey explodes back into life at the most important lock along England's oldest canal – the Fossdyke. This 11 mile waterway was excavated by the Romans to link the River Witham in Lincoln with the Trent at Torksey. Today the canal is dedicated to leisure craft, and the basin around the huge walls of the lock has become a marina. Continue south as the road sweeps to the left until, ½ mile later, you **turn L** into an unmarked lane just past a small stream. This brings you through the village of Fenton and back to the main road at the Carpenters Arms. **Turn R**, immediately **turn L** (signed 'Kettlethorpe'), and at a small crossroads continue ahead (signed 'Kettlethorpe') along a lane twisting and turning into the exquisite hamlet of Kettlethorpe.

Having absorbed all that historic Kettlethorpe has to offer return to the small crossroads, **turn L** (signed 'Laughterton'), and then **turn R** in Laughterton itself (signed 'Gainsborough'), where you see an

RAF memorial on the village green in the form of a single mounted propeller blade. You soon regain the A156 at the White Swan, handsomely painted black and white, and you **turn L** (signed 'Gainsborough'). This time travel north until you come to the village sign for Torksey. Opposite this **turn R** into Sand Lane, a charming byway which brings you to a junction at the Gatekeeper's Cottage. **Turn R** here, then **turn R** again when you reach a signpost for Hardwick. Now relax, for this road meanders this way and that across open countryside, as it leads you for 3 miles, all the way back into the heart of Saxilby.

Stow Minster

SAXILBY

Boats and barges on the Fossdyke today give Saxilby the feel of a holiday village, and the grassy canal banks reward exploration, especially around the brick remains of the demolished swingbridge. In 1936 it was in Saxilby that the Jarrow marchers rested on their desperate trek to Westminster to save their shipyards. They were cold, exhausted, unfed and unshod. The ladies of Saxilby rallied round to provide food, water and blankets, while the cobblers in the village repaired their footwear. The next morning the marchers were sent warmly on their way, reclothed and revived.

STOW MINSTER

The origins of Saint Mary's Minster are shrouded in mystery, but the building certainly dates from 1034, when it was the mother church of West Lindsey. Mighty Saxon arches have been bolstered by Gothic additions, and the spacious Norman chancel is breathtaking. Enriched by Lady Godiva and Bishop Remigius, the building predates Lincoln Cathedral by hundreds of years.

KETTLETHORPE

Kettlethorpe is famous as the home of Lady Katherine Swynford, third wife of John of Gaunt and heroine of Anya Seton's historical novel *Katherine*. Today all that remains of the original Hall is a huge arched stone gateway in front of its present incarnation, and a section of the moat. These and other buildings are delightfully set around the shaded grounds of the restored church.

5

The Villages and Churches of the North Wolds

28 miles

If you are suffering from the misapprehension that Lincolnshire is a flat county then this is the ride that will cure you. Completely rural, the route descends to the eastern coastal plain, then doubles back across the entire breadth of the hilly Wolds, almost as far as the western escarpment, before returning to the starting point. However, a quick glance at the map shows that there are numerous ways of reducing the distance. Otherwise this is a full day's outing, and you are urged to take your time and explore fully the many sleepy villages you will visit. Sheltering in each of these villages is a church of distinction, and in most cases a surprisingly noble hall – a throwback to a more regal era when land and farming went hand in hand with riches and grandeur.

Map: OS Landranger 113 Grimsby (GR 210939).

Starting point: The Market Square in Binbrook, which is on the B1203 midway between Market Rasen and Grimsby. Ample street parking is available but there is no railway serving this area.

Refreshments: Although there are only a few refreshment outlets, there are many stunning picnic spots, for which you may wish to make provision. However the Plough at Binbrook, Swinhope's Clickem Inn and the Nickerson Arms in Rothwell and are all excellent, and all serve food. In addition Roosters Bistro in Ashby-cum-Fenby is situated just off-route, as are inns in North Thoresby and Holton-le-Clay.

Leave the trim brick and colour-washed houses around Binbrook's attractive cobbled Market Square to pass the Plough Inn on your right, and round a corner to reach the first of the day's churches, St Mary and St Gabriel's. Climb out of the village and **turn L** (signed 'Ludborough'). A mile further on **turn L** at one 'Give Way' sign, and **turn R** at another. Continue over the next crossroads (signed 'North Thoresby') and climb out of this wooded dip to Beesby Top Farm, passing a procession of curious tree stumps resembling the remains of some ancient henge. Beyond the farm **turn R** over a cattle-grid towards Cadeby Farm and follow the firm track all the way around the estate and along an avenue of tall elms. Spot the remains of an octagonal brick dovecote on your right, and then, beyond a huge spreading cedar, the

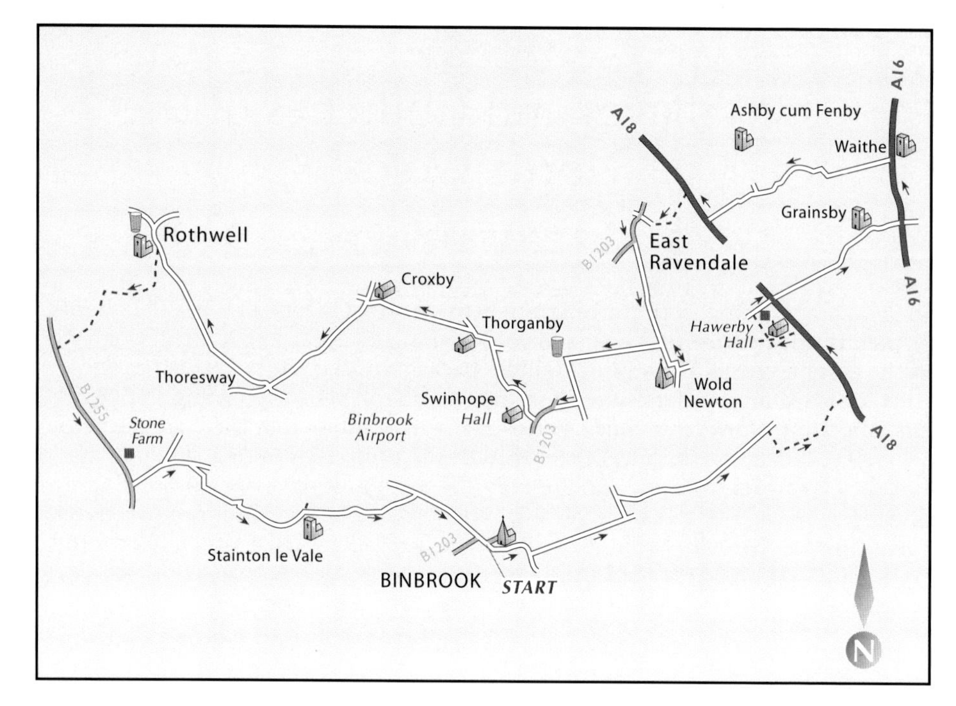

splendid but now derelict hulk of Cadeby Hall. The track leads you to the A18 (the Barton Street), onto which you **turn L**.

In ¾ mile **turn L** onto a bridleway at a lodge and you soon pass a diminutive church, wonderfully sited, but in a sad state of decay. When the track, now grassy, enters open fields, **turn R** along the hedge to follow the bridleway towards a rank of tall trees and another lodge. At the road **turn R** and continue down the hill towards Grainsby, crossing the Barton Street with care. Here you enter a delightful scene, a stretch of beautiful fenced and gated parkland. Reaching the estate village of Grainsby it is not only the castellated tower of St Nicholas' church which attracts attention – every building in the hamlet seems to catch the eye.

Turn L when you arrive at the main A16 (signed 'Grimsby'), then **turn R** at the next crossroads into the tiny hamlet of Waithe. Having inspected the estate cottages and the tall but now disused and haunting church, return to the crossroads. This time continue straight over (signed 'Brigsley') to follow a winding lane with excellent open views until, at the top of the hill, you **turn R** to rejoin the Barton Street (signed 'Immingham'). In ⅓ mile **turn L** where you see a green bridleway, and climb to the top, passing woods on either side. Looking over your shoulder the view now

extends down over the whole of the coastal plain to the Humber estuary, Spurn Point Lighthouse and the North Sea beyond. **Turn R** when the track reaches a lane, immediately **turn L** where the bridleway disappears behind 'The Elms' then **turn R** again onto the next lane. You now find yourself in East Ravendale where you pass a series of interesting buildings to your right – including a restored thatched mud-and-stud cottage – as you descend to the B1203. **Turn L** (signed 'Binbrook') and, having rounded a duckpond in the grounds of Ravendale Hall, **turn L** again (signed 'Wold Newton') and follow this road for a mile.

Wold Newton is well worth exploring as far as All Saints' church – approached, naturally enough, through the garden gates of Church Path Cottage. Retrace your route as far as a signpost for Swinhope and **turn L** here. **Turn L** at the next junction (signed 'Kelstern'), and after ½ mile **turn R** (signed 'Swinhope'). This downhill lane offers you a superb view over the whole of the basin that gives Stainton-le-Vale and Kirmond-le-Mire their names. But care is required as you **turn L** to join the B1203 (signed 'Binbrook') and shortly after **turn R** (signed 'Swinhope'). Now a short detour will give you the chance to enjoy Swinhope's ancient church, set between pink confectionery cottages and houses, and boasting a splendid view of Swinhope Hall from its porch. Leaving Swinhope, sneak a glance back at the swans on the lake in front of the Hall as you continue along the unfenced lane overlooking the brook to your left.

After a mile you reach Thorganby, another tiny village with another tiny church. **Turn L** at the next fork (signed 'Croxby') and, as you climb out of Thorganby, look back across the valley to gain the best view of Thorganby Hall over the treetops. The next mile is steep and you will find it difficult to believe that the runway for the old airfield at Binbrook was built on the land directly to your left. Soon enough, however, the rooftops of the hamlet of Croxby become visible, and you hurtle down to the bridge over the stream which meanders through gardens towards the impressive Croxby Hall. Passing All Saints', the smallest of churches, continue to the brow of the hill, **turn L** (signed 'Thoresway'), and enjoy the next mile to the full. Reasonably level, this section offers intimate views over ponds and meadows as it follows the sylvan valley of the tree-lined stream below.

At the crossroads, you should stray into Thoresway and meander through the village before returning to this point. **Turn L** (signed 'Rothwell') and, enjoying good views back over Thoresway, ascend the hill. A mile further on you plummet towards the picturesque village of Rothwell, which you will wish to spend some time exploring. Leave Rothwell by the same road but, where the stream goes underneath the road opposite a conifer hedge, spot a tarmac bridleway leading towards a large willow and **turn R** onto it. You are now entering the highlight of the route and a secret which really should not be shared, a lane winding through the private estate established by Joseph Nickerson in 1951 and named the 'Great Walk'. To your right a beautiful stream gurgles over waterfalls and through ponds full of bulrushes. Past a larger lake and several narrow wooded strips the track begins to regain height and, passing Rothwell Top Farm, reaches Caistor High Street at another farm.

Turn L and follow this busier road for 1½ miles. Here you are at the highest point of the route and on the western edge of the Wolds. Having passed the distinctive silos and crenellated outbuildings of Stone Farm **turn L** (signed 'Thoresway') and, at the end of a row of huge gnarled beech trees, **turn R** (signed 'Stainton-le-Vale'). Around a bend the narrow road drops steeply towards Stainton Hall Farm, set amid lawns, streams, a lake and brick estate buildings all neatly trimmed in scarlet. Through the farm the stream and road continue past more huge beeches towards the tiny village of Stainton-le-Vale itself, and beyond to the final church you will visit – St Andrews, with its squat stone tower.

At the next fork **turn R** (signed 'Binbrook'). This mile is something of a switchback but offers fine views over the contours of the unfenced cornfields, the valleys and the areas of woodland which are the essence of the Wolds. Finally, having passed Priory Farm on your right, **turn R** at a large junction and you are less than a mile from your starting point in the Market Square in Binbrook.

THORESWAY

The tall narrow whitewashed building was in fact a watermill built in 1816, but with two unusual features. Water for the mill was supplied by a raised channel entering the building at roof level, gaining enough height to feed the overshot wheel. In addition the mill itself contained no apparatus – the power was taken under the road to drive machinery in the farm buildings opposite.

ROTHWELL

Three wooded valleys lead to the picturesque village of Rothwell, where a clear brook flows over a stony bed between the road and interesting clusters of brick farm buildings opposite the impressive long white façade of the village inn. It was in this village that Joseph Nickerson, a renowned plant breeder and experimental farmer, based his seed empire. Knighted for his services to agriculture in 1983, Sir Joseph died in 1990, but his impact on the surrounding countryside is unmistakable. The fields he owned are lined by immaculately trimmed hedges and verges, with daffodils and wildflowers abundant. His concern for nature conservation is nowhere more focused than around the 'Great Walk'.

6

The Woods and Wolds around Tealby

20 miles

The Lincolnshire Wolds are not noted for attractive stone-built villages – Tealby is the exception and the perfect base for a day's cycling. Houses of mellow local ironstone cluster around the fords, mills and waterfalls of the River Rase. Your route begins and ends in the rolling Wolds foothills, but in between a captivating trip through fields and forests on a variety of surfaces links the ancestral home of the Heneage squires with a tiny village of two churches, each fascinating for different reasons.

Maps: OS Landranger 113 Grimsby, 121 Lincoln & Newark-on-Trent and a very short stretch on 122 Skegness & Horncastle (GR 158908).

Starting point: The free car park at the Tennyson D'Eyncourt Memorial Hall in Tealby. Tealby is north-east of Market Rasen on the B1203 to Grimsby. Turn south at the church and a few yards down the hill the hall is clearly visible on the left.

Refreshments: Apart from those mentioned in Tealby, refreshment opportunities are few, with only the Heneage Arms in Hainton and the kiosk at Willingham Woods offering you sustenance along the way. However, the town of Market Rasen is only a couple of miles off-route.

Out of the car park, past the Tennyson D'Eyncourt Memorial Hall and directly into Front Street, you are immediately surrounded by some of Tealby's treasures. To your right All Saints' church commands a supreme view of the whole village, to your left Beck Hill leads through a ford to Bayons Park where once would have stood the romantic folly of Bayons Manor, while ahead of you lies the Gothic school building, not unlike the Great Hall of Bayons itself. And that's not the toughest decision that Tealby presents to you. Will you choose a meal in one of the two excellent public houses? Or a cream tea and a portion of homemade gateau from the Tealby Tearooms? Maybe you'll just prepare for a picnic with a pork pie and a slice of plum loaf (both Lincolnshire made, naturally) from the tiny butcher's shop at the bottom of Front Street, renowned as the home of Lincolnshire's finest sausages!

Front Street leads into Cow Lane and, after passing the thatched King's Head, **turn L** into Sandy Lane (signed 'North Willingham'). Do not miss an exquisite view to your left, where the River Rase cascades from a hidden millpond down the side of a golden stone cottage, formerly one of Tealby's numerous watermills. The lane now meanders out of the village, passing a side road heading for Tealby Thorpe, also a picture postcard scene, with another ford near another watermill – this brief diversion is recommended. Eventually Sandy Lane reaches the main A631, at which you **turn L** (signed 'North Willingham') and join a shared cycle lane as far as North Willingham, where you **turn R** (signed 'Sixhills').

Survey the earthworks of a 12th century Gilbertine priory on your right before embarking on an ascent which betrays the origin of the name of the next village, Sixhills. Continue through the village enjoying views towards Lincoln Cathedral on the skyline to the right. On your left rolling arable fields slope down to wooded valleys, into one of which you tumble and rise to arrive at the village of Hainton.

Hainton is more conspicuously an estate village, doors and wooden facings neatly picked out in bright red. When you reach the top of the village, where a stone lodge with a Jacobean turret faces the Heneage Arms, turn and backtrack to a side road (signed 'East Torrington') at which you **turn L**. Here the best view of the church's elegant slender spire is unveiled, at the end of a narrow shaded lane from where the only sight of Hainton's secluded Hall is possible. But your route continues past the densely wooded grounds to a lane bearing only a 'Public Bridleway' sign. **Turn R** onto this and hurtle down the hillside to begin an adventurous passage through idyllic countryside.

The lane becomes a chalky track and reaches a bend where 'Public Bridleway' signs point in two directions. You, however, **turn L** here onto an unsigned 'green lane', a wide grassy path guided by hedgerows on both sides. Continue ahead onto a firmer track joining you from Clump Hill Farm on your left and adhere to this when it bends through gates to the right. This byway now guides you all the way to Little London, no more than a cluster of farms. **Turn R** at the T-junction and, where the road spins sharply left, **turn R** onto a forest track (signed as a public byway) leading to a delightful clearing. Do not follow the track between the buildings of Dog Kennel Farm, but hug the rails of the horse paddock to join a grassy track through the forest. This enchanting trail emerges at a field-side, which it follows beneath a treetop canopy to the busy A631.

Cross carefully and **turn L** along a cycle track which follows the barely discernible stone boundary wall of the now-vanished Willingham Hall as far as another forest clearing, a popular spot with a car park and a

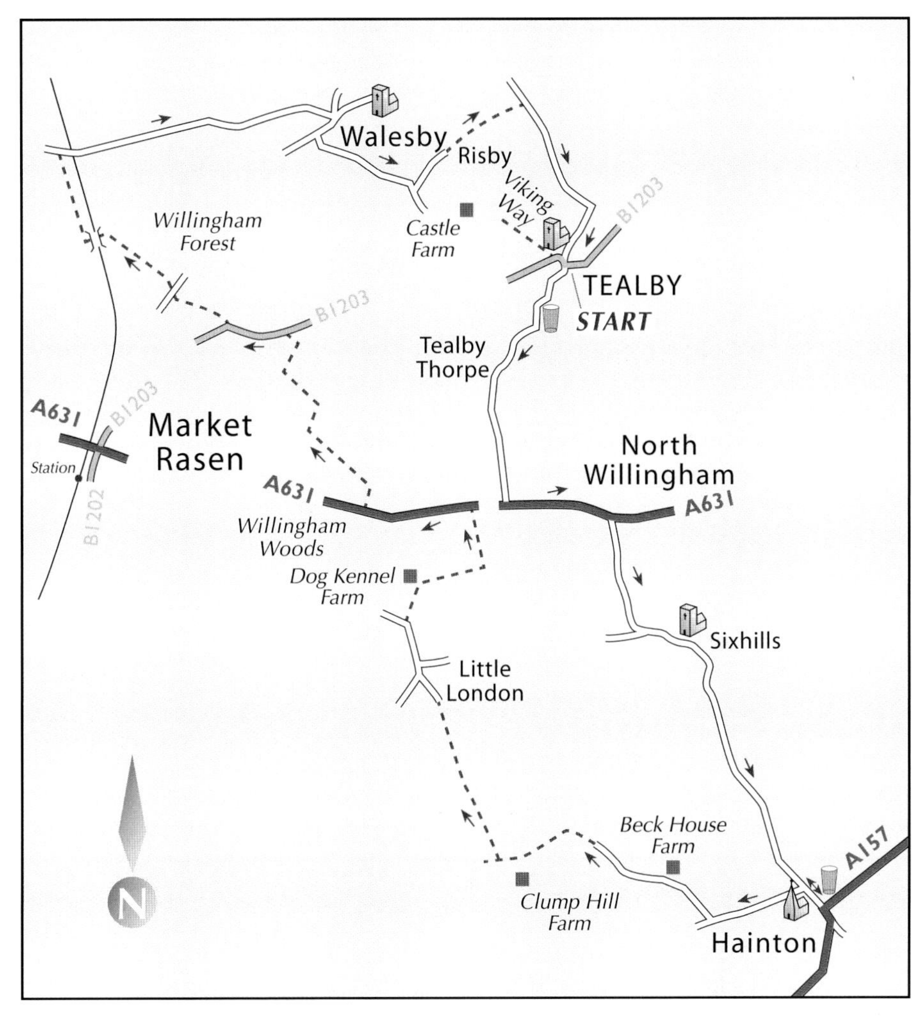

refreshment kiosk. At a gateway at the far end of this layby, **turn R** onto a stony track, one of many paths and cycle-ways that criss-cross Willingham Woods. At the first major junction **turn L**, and after ½ mile **turn R** at the converted brick offices of the Forestry Commission. Pass a farm cottage and a clearing on your right, and continue ahead as far as a another junction, where your way ahead is prohibited. **Turn R** here and, keeping to the main track, you eventually emerge at a road.

Turn L and follow this road along the lower slopes of Hamilton Hill, in the woods to your left. This hill is the place where rebel forces congregated during the futile Lincolnshire Uprising of 1536, their doomed gesture earning them only a royal slur, the dismissal of Lincolnshire folk as 'the most brutal and beastly of our realm'. Soon you spot a track just in front of Poplar Farm (a public byway) onto which you **turn R**. Lined with oak and gorse this sandy track soon reaches a forest road, which you cross. Pass a caravan park on your right and continue ahead until your track arrives at the red brick arch of Nova Scotia Bridge. Crossing over the bridge you are guided to the right, and another sandy trail leads you through gorse and bracken to the next road, onto which you **turn R** and double back over the railway lines.

Open views over the Wolds now accompany you all the way into Walesby, with the 12th century Ramblers' church prominent. In the village **turn R** when you spot the new village hall on your left, and immediately **turn R** again (signed 'Tealby'). Passing the new parish church of Saint Mary and All Saints you **turn L** (signed 'Tealby') into Catskin Lane, and follow this to a junction with a public bridleway. **Turn L** here to cross a cattle grid and ascend the steep incline, passing a row of sturdy horse chestnuts. Admire an imposing stone-dressed hall as you follow the track through the farming hamlet of Risby, beyond which a somewhat bumpier surface crosses two fields to reach a lonely high-level lane near a large barn. **Turn R** here for a thrilling finale to the ride. As you pass a series of tall beeches, curiously weathered to identical profiles by the elements, unbeatable views stretch across the valley as far as Lincoln and the River Trent. Suddenly the road bends to the right and nosedives towards Tealby, between the trim stone cottages lining Caistor Lane and the churchyard's glowing new drystone wall. Cross Papermill Lane with great care (signed 'North Willingham'), and cruise once more into the car park behind Tealby's village hall.

BAYONS MANOR

In 1835 Charles Tennyson D'Eyncourt, an uncle of Alfred, Lord Tennyson, inherited a modest manor in Tealby's Bayons Park. He converted his new home into a huge romantic Gothic folly, a castle complete with moat, drawbridge and portcullis. Today only a few walls remain amidst dense trees, after the army blew up what was left of the decaying ruin in 1965.

HAINTON

Saint Mary's, the family church of the Heneages – owners of the neighbouring Hall since the 14th century – paints a striking enough portrait when approached from the nearby lane. But beneath the spire is a greater wealth, a collection of tombs and monuments to the Heneages dating from 1435 to the present day. This rich gallery combines marble, alabaster, brass and radiant colours in a chapel enclosed by iron gates. The grounds of the Hall were redesigned by Capability Brown.

7

The Louth Navigational Canal

25 miles

Louth is renowned as a market town of the rolling Wolds, but in truth to the east looks over a vast area of low level farmland. The abandoned Louth Navigational Canal crosses this coastal 'marsh' to connect with the North Sea at Tetney, and makes an ideal guide for a trip towards the coast. Atmospheric views of Louth's spire on the horizon dominate throughout, and in winter this journey can even be extended to include a fascinating wildlife experience. Starting and finishing at the welcoming and refreshing Navigation Warehouse at the end of the former canal, the route, which includes some off-road work, is level throughout.

Map: OS Landranger 113 Grimsby (GR 337879).

Starting point: The Riverhead in Louth, 16 miles south of Grimsby on the A16 (no train service). From near Saint James' spire in the centre of Louth head along Eastgate and, in ¾ mile turn left into Riverhead Road, and you will see the Riverhead on your right. There is parking at the Navigation Warehouse and ample street parking in the area.

Refreshments: Of all Louth's many refreshment facilities the Navigation Warehouse teashop ranks among the best. En route, Covenham's Mill House is also first class, while good inns at Marshchapel, Grainthorpe and North Somercotes also serve food – and don't miss the home-made ice-cream at Conisholme!

From the Navigation Warehouse head past the Woolpack and along Ramsgate Road to the swimming pool, where you **turn R** into Victoria Road. A slight incline (the only one of the day) leads past a crossroads where you continue ahead (signed 'Yarburgh') until you exit Louth at the sign depicting Saint Herefrid. Good views begin to open up over the Wolds and the coastal plain, while behind you the spire of Saint James' in Louth, though impressive, is dwarfed by a colossal maltings building.

The road now seems to zigzag interminably, passing the entrance drive to Brackenborough Hall, the site of an ancient medieval village. Beyond Brackenborough Wood on your left and one more bend to the right, you reach a clear side road, unsigned at the time of writing, into which you **turn L**. This new lane crosses a shaded brook and

Watching the seals at Donna Nook

passes a farm before more zigzags lead you finally into Covenham, a straggling but attractive village, with ranges of cottages and farm buildings and two very close though contrasting churches. Saint Mary's is tall and elegant, cared for and welcoming, while the redundant Saint Bartholomew's crumbles away beneath a canopy of yews in its overgrown atmospheric yard – one the home of joyful celebration, the other of spiritual solemnity.

Meandering past the Plough on the left the road leaves the village, veering at the picturesque thatch of the excellent Mill House Restaurant before arriving at a crossroads. Here **turn R** onto Firebeacon Lane (signed 'Grainthorpe') and pass the grassy ramparts of Covenham Reservoir. An ascent of the banks is recommended to gain a wonderful panorama of the surrounding lowlands, stretching as far as the Dock Tower in Grimsby. At last you rejoin the Louth Canal at a farm where, bizarrely, two large nosy dinosaurs peer at you over a boatyard hedge. Over the bridge **turn L** (unsigned) and follow the canal now on your left, until the lane leads you abruptly to the right towards Marshchapel.

Here you are at once greeted by an unusually imposing church, Saint Mary's, embattled and pinnacled,

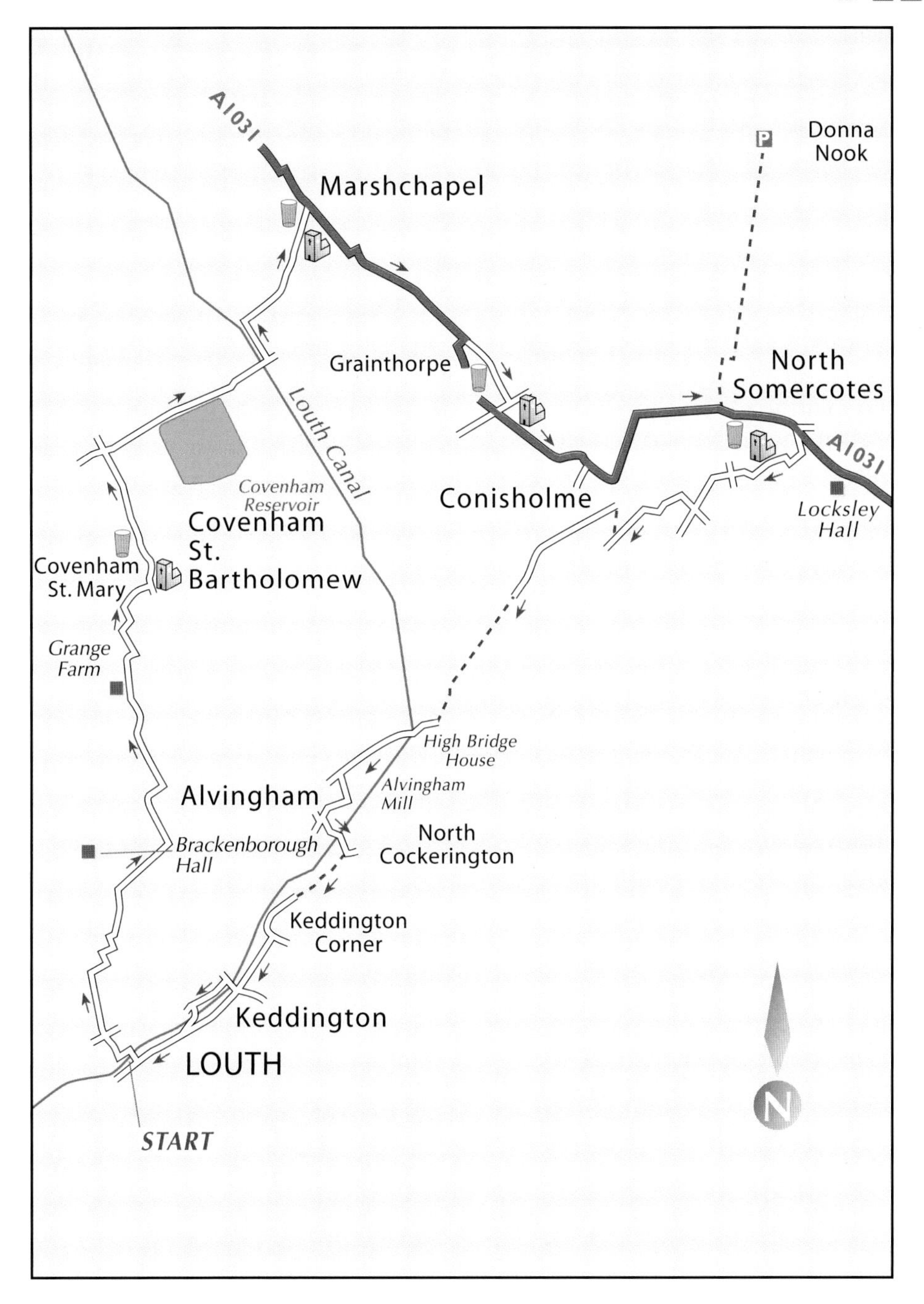
A1031
Donna Nook
Marshchapel
Grainthorpe
North Somercotes
Louth Canal
Covenham Reservoir
Conisholme
A1031
Locksley Hall
Covenham St. Bartholomew
Covenham St. Mary
Grange Farm
High Bridge House
Alvingham Mill
Alvingham
North Cockerington
Brackenborough Hall
Keddington Corner
Keddington
LOUTH
START
N

and known as the 'Cathedral of the Marsh'. Hideous gargoyles high on the tower and a remarkable display of 134 different wooden pew heads, all crafted by the same woodcarver, are of particular interest. Beneath a yew tree you may also spot a sad row of 19 little unmarked graves. Mary Loft, who lived in the village's Old Hall in the 18th century, had 19 children – all of whom died in infancy. Reaching the main road through Marshchapel you will deduce that the main part of the village lies to your left, and is well worth exploring. The route, however, is in the opposite direction and you **turn R** (signed 'Grainthorpe') to proceed carefully along the A1031.

After 2 miles, at a war memorial in Grainthorpe, **turn L** into High Street to fully appreciate this village, passing interesting groups of brick buildings before steering around a fenced paddock. Soon this delightful lane angles right, with the 16th century Tithe Farm on your left heralding another majestic marshland church tower, before rejoining the main coastal road. **Turn L** here (signed 'Conisholme'). Having been suitably delayed by Appleby's Famous Farm Ices, 2 more miles lead you into the typical scattered coastal village of North Somercotes. From here any of three well-signed roads on your left will lead you 2 miles further on to the sandy dunes at Donna Nook, the winter breeding grounds of the grey seals.

Continue to explore North Somercotes as far as Locksley Hall on your right, dating from the 16th century, and famed as the subject of Tennyson's poem of the same name.

From the Hall double back to a disused schoolyard on the left, at which you **turn L** into School Lane (signed 'Church End'). Adhere to this lane as it winds along a secluded leafy section by the church, go straight ahead at a crossroads (signed 'Conisholme') and prepare for a test of your navigational skills. **Turn R** at the unsigned T-junction at Eau Bridge Farm, and, where the road forks, **turn L** (signed 'North Somercotes Fen') to continue for ½ mile to the next farm on the left. Beyond this farm look carefully on the right for the next field boundary. Dismount, **turn R** and walk along this unmarked bridleway with the fence on your right and an aluminium bar gate as your target, a distance of less than 100 yards. The gate is soon gained – remount and **turn R** along the grassy track before you, which improves gradually until you emerge in Conisholme again, alongside the tiny church.

Turn L here and head once more into the remote depths of these agricultural expanses. Quite simply your route now forges directly ahead, although the terrain changes continuously. Tarmac gives way to chalk to grass and back to tarmac again 2 miles later, where

you reacquaint yourself with the canal at High Bridge. Soon you **turn L** into a side road opposite the sign for High Bridge Road, and Abbey Road leads you down the hill to Alvingham. At the T-junction **turn L** to view the churches and the handsome watermill, then return to the junction and continue straight on to pass through Alvingham. At a junction with a superior road **turn L** (signed 'North Cockerington'), cross the canal again at an old disused lock, and **turn R** onto a grassy byway where the road bends to the left.

This track undulates above the canal for a mile until you reach a firm surface next to a house. **Turn L** here then **turn R** onto a main road at Keddington Corner. At the tree-clad site of the former Louth Park Abbey on your left, **turn R** (signed 'Alvingham'), cross the canal at Ticklepenny Lock, and immediately **turn L** (unsigned) at a petanque piste into the narrowest of lanes, to continue with a paddock and the canal now on your left. Cowslip Lane leads you into a picturesque hamlet called Keddington, where you **turn L** into River Lane, and at the foot of the hill locate a tiny wicket gate opening onto a footpath through the meadow on your left. Dismount once more as this short stroll leads you to the most striking section of the entire canal, where the serene shaded waters suddenly plunge over the walls of the disused Keddington Lock.

Over the canal bridge **turn R** and follow a short delightful stretch of the towpath. **Turn L** over another footbridge, easily detected, which brings you onto Eastfield Road, where you may remount. **Turn R** and when you see Riverhead Road, **turn R** again, and there at the foot of the hill is the welcoming teashop and the end of the ride.

THE LOUTH NAVIGATIONAL CANAL

This 12-mile waterway was opened in 1770 and its most remarkable features are its lock walls, shaped like a series of barrels to keep back the marshy surrounding land. Ticklepenny Lock is named after the lockkeeper, whose family's graves can be found in Keddington churchyard. The ailing canal was finally abandoned in 1924, but exciting plans are afoot to reopen it. The Navigation Warehouse at the Riverhead mainly stored wool and grain, and has been painstakingly restored as a restaurant and a series of display areas.

DONNA NOOK

Donna Nook, like nearby Rimac and the Prussian Queen inn at Saltfleetby, takes its name from a ship once wrecked on its desolate shores, which are now well known as an RAF bombing range. But since the 1970s these dunes and mudflats have served as an important breeding ground. Each November and December hundreds of grey seals – the largest wild mammal in Britain – come ashore, the cows giving birth to their pups, and then mating with the waiting bulls to begin the cycle again. This extraordinary natural occurrence attracts visitors in their droves.

8

Louth: Mills and Streams on the Edge of the Wolds

23 miles

Starting in the shadow of one of the country's finest church spires in the thriving market town of Louth, here is a route which takes you through every type of countryside that Lincolnshire has to offer. Following a number of streams running down from the Wolds you will enjoy watermills and windmills, castles and churches, even railways and runways, before these watercourses meander away across the coastal plain to the North Sea.

Map: OS Landranger 122 Skegness & Horncastle (GR 327873).

Starting point: Saint James' church in central Louth, 16 miles south of Grimsby on the A16. You should use signed car parks in Louth itself, as there is only limited street parking. Although you will spend the day crossing many former rail routes, Louth is no longer blessed with a train service.

Refreshments: Restaurants and inns abound in Louth. Along the route, after the excellent 'Splash' in Little Cawthorpe there are no inns until Manby, although tearooms at Claythorpe or at Greenways on the A157 may cater for your needs. You will also find several inns in villages just off the route.

From Saint James' church head south along Upgate as far as the traffic lights, at which you **turn L** into Newmarket (signed 'Mablethorpe'), to pass the indoor cattle market and the proud theatre of the Louth Playgoers on your right. Continue for 3 miles until you arrive at the village of Legbourne, negotiating on the way a busy roundabout, and spotting a smart lodge guarding Kenwick Hall and Legbourne's old brick station building, until recently a museum.

The village of Legbourne is handsome enough, the distinctive chalk walls and green copper roof of All Saints' church rising behind a canopied Gothic drinking fountain. Opposite this scene **turn R** into Mill Lane and cross the course of the old Louth to Boston railway, a victim of Doctor Beeching in the 1960s. Now pass another group of fine buildings where a huge windmill is coupled with a watermill, a very rare combination as technical limitations meant that wind and water power could not be used simultaneously. Today the site has been restored as one of many

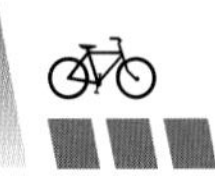

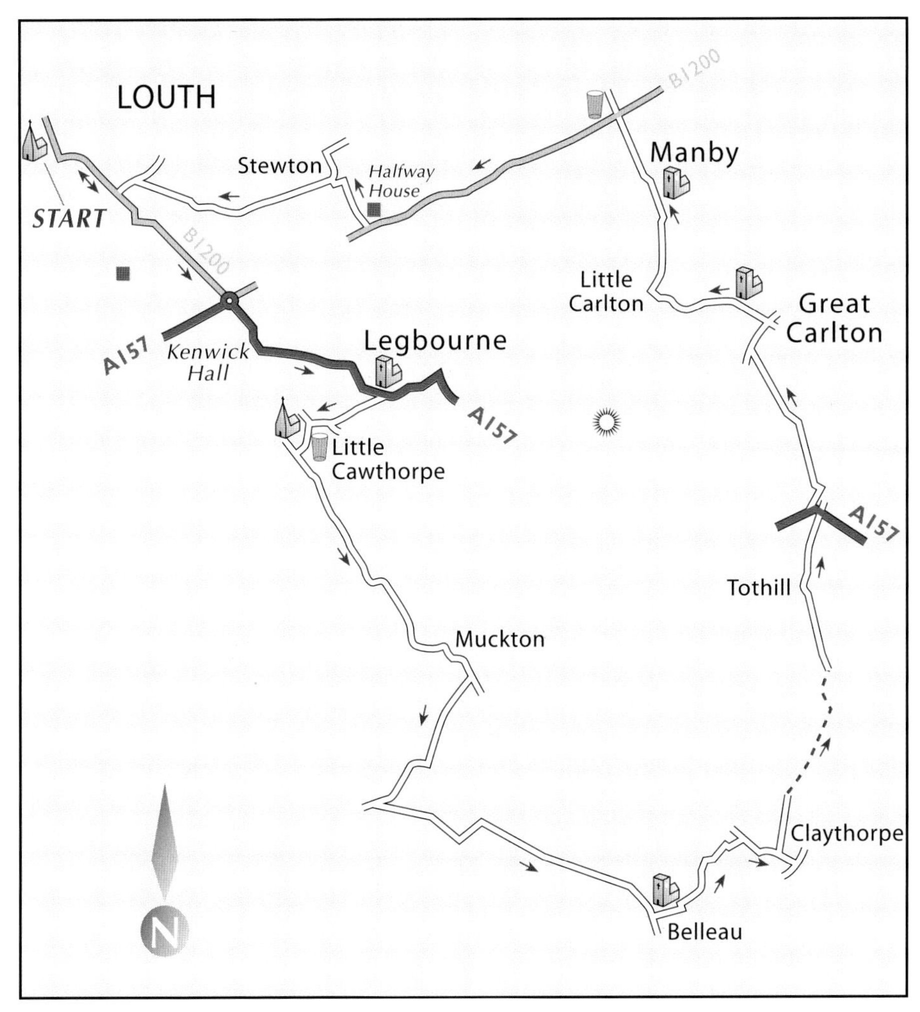

trout farms in the area around Louth.

Now you come across a most beguiling scene, where the lane and the river bed of the Long Eau unite for several hundred yards. Beckside, a raised footpath shaded by trees on both banks, runs alongside and crosses the stream twice on narrow footbridges. You should dismount and walk your cycle along this section, a delay which should be seen as a blessing. The waters run crystal-clear over the pebbles, and just to complete this perfect rural vision you emerge at another ford overlooked by the lawns of a country inn – named the Royal Oak, but known to all as 'The Splash'. Out of the inn driveway **turn L** into Little

Cawthorpe and the twisting lane will bring you to a charming duckpond set in a hollow on your right. All around you can hear springs and waterfalls rushing down to join the stream, and from a hillside above, the pretty red and black brick church, Saint Helen's, surveys the scene.

At the nearby junction facing the 17th century Manor House, **turn L** into Muckton Road. Now the nature of the ride alters dramatically, as you climb along the side of the Wolds, with views opening up across the coastal 'marsh' as far as Mablethorpe, and Legbourne's windmill and church now prominent behind you. Two miles further on, having slalomed through the farming hamlet of Muckton, **turn R** where you see an enormous copper beech (signed 'Burwell'). Heading higher into the Wolds the road re-enters wooded territory, and having passed through the aptly named Dark Lane Plantation, look carefully and **turn L** (signed 'South Thoresby'). On your left here a curious walled garden and derelict corner-house are superseded by a series of narrow lakes set among tall alders.

After another ascent **turn R** when you see a sign for Belleau and follow this lane to Meagram Top. Continue straight on (signed 'Belleau') onto the superior road and proceed to a white cottage above the village of Belleau at which you **turn L** onto an unsigned road. Now apply your brakes as you speed downhill or you will miss Belleau's chalk and greenstone church tower and an intriguing octagonal Tudor dovecote on your right. The route twists undecidedly to a T-junction – **turn R** here and continue into Claythorpe, passing a couple of interesting old railway buildings. When you reach the bridge over the deeply wooded Great Eau, you can see to your right the quite delightful tower and chimneys of Claythorpe Mill, and you will wish to spend time exploring the site.

Now backtrack through Claythorpe until you spot the entrance drive up to the Hall on your left, and opposite this is a tarmac road simply signed 'public bridleway' and 'dead end'. **Turn R** onto this lane which deteriorates to a firm chalky track, but is still an exciting short-cut across open country, leading you eventually to the moated ramparts of a modest motte and bailey castle, now merely an evocative tree-covered mound. The path circles the earthworks to the left before rejoining a metalled surface at a farmyard, from which peacocks and geese will watch you cycle away. **Turn R** (signed 'Alford') at a junction in Tothill and, reaching the main A157, **turn L** (signed 'Louth'), then **turn R** into the second side-road (signed 'Carlton').

This road leads you all the way into Great Carlton where you **turn L** at

the only crossroads (signed 'Little Carlton'), and pass on your right two impressive brick halls and the restored 15th century church tower, bearing unusual mounted stone tablets inscribed with prayers for the souls of the church's benefactors. Continue into Little Carlton, a village of no church but still boasting a fine three-storey watermill building and, a mile to the south, the overgrown earthworks of another small castle.

Remain on the same road to pass through Manby, the houses immediately marking it out as an RAF base, abandoned but redeveloped for a variety of modern uses. At the traffic lights **turn L** onto the B1200 (signed 'Louth') and pass the entire length of the airfield, as well as a large military tank, suitably forbidding if incongruous on airforce land. Now, drawn by magnificent views of the spire in Louth, continue for a mile beyond the end of the runways to **turn R** onto an unsigned lane where Halfway House is situated on the corner. This lane brings you into Stewton, an entirely agricultural settlement, and it is well worth following a sign to the tiny hidden Norman church on the right. From the church return to Stewton's Old Railway House, and continue straight ahead on a leafy lane with the abandoned railway bed on your left. The occasional outposts of civilisation gradually increase to a suburban hubbub, and, if you **turn L** at the first T-junction then **turn R** at the second, you find yourself back in Newmarket, with less than a mile between you and Louth town centre.

LOUTH

The undisputed capital of the Wolds, Louth's finest feature is the Gothic spire of Saint James' church, soaring to a height of 295 ft. Louth's proud religious history dates back to the founding of a Cistercian abbey at Louth Park in 1139, but the town has also had more than its fair share of adversity. The abbey fell to the Dissolution in 1536, but the uprising by the townspeople that followed suffered an even more gruesome fate, with several of them hanged at Tyburn Gallows, including the vicar, Thomas Kendall. During the plague in 1651 the town lost 747 people in that year alone, and more recently 29 people were killed in 1920 when the swollen waters of the River Lud swept through the town.

CLAYTHORPE

Now gleaming white, the listed three-storey Claythorpe Mill was built from brick at the start of the 19th century to harness the power of the Great Eau for corn milling. Although the wheel no longer turns the site has been carefully restored to include an exhibition of bygones, tearooms, trout ponds and an outstanding collection of unusual waterfowl and other creatures.

The Bluestone Heath Road

26 miles

Sweeping along the crest of the Lincolnshire Wolds, this is an exhilarating ride on an ancient drove road offering thrilling views over the valleys below. In addition to the Bluestone Heath Road, your circuit links four 'icing-sugar Gothic' churches, medieval in appearance but actually designed by the same Louth architect in the 19th century. Steep gradients and an adventurous off-road section are included before the day's finale is reached, the quite stunning setting of Biscathorpe – the perfect picnic stop!

Map: OS Landranger 122 Skegness & Horncastle (GR 236829).

Starting point: St Andrew's church in Donington-on-Bain, which is situated 2 miles south-east of the intersection of the B1225 Horncastle to Caistor 'High Street' and the A157 linking Louth and Lincoln. Donington is clearly signposted from both roads, and you will have no trouble parking around the village – the local shopkeeper may allow you to park in the yard by the shop.

Refreshments: Only the excellent Black Horse and village shop in Donington-on-Bain offer you any chance of refreshment, although good inns in Scamblesby and Tetford are just off-route, and at one point you pass within a couple of miles of Louth. If you opt for a picnic – Biscathorpe is an unbeatable spot!

From the squat tower of Saint Andrew's church in Donington-on-Bain advance south past the Black Horse Inn and leave the village, passing an extraordinary old wooden dwelling on your left. A fine prospect immediately opens out to the wooded slopes of the Wolds, and you continue along the Bain valley until you reach the neat church of Saint Nicholas, set behind a trimmed hedge and dwarfed by a large beech. **Turn L** here (signed 'Raithby') and ascend steeply into the woods, struggling for a view of the secluded Stenigot House on your left, but admiring the lead tower of the handsome stable block opposite. As this lane levels out, pass another range of impressive high-gabled farm buildings before you **turn L** at one junction (signed 'Raithby'), then **turn R** at another (signed 'Scamblesby').

You are now riding the Bluestone Heath Road, here exposed and treeless, but offering glimpses of Louth's soaring spire along the valleys to your left. When you reach a major crossroads, cross

The watermill at Donington-on-Bain

carefully and continue ahead (signed 'Belchford'). You may have heard the growing roar of opening throttles from some way back – now you realise why as you come alongside Cadwell Park motor racing circuit, in jarring contrast to these tranquil rural surroundings. Proceed along the Bluestone Heath Road into a greener landscape, with a series of lush valleys to your left and a huge panoramic outlook below you to the right.

Reaching a sign for Oxcombe, **turn L** towards this peaceful hamlet to visit All Saints', the first of the day's connected churches, approached past the arches and turrets of Oxcombe House and along a sheltered grassy swathe. Return and **turn L** onto the Bluestone Heath Road once more, and in a further 1½ miles, **turn L** again (signed 'Ruckland'). At this point a brief glance at an Ordnance Survey map shows that the route could easily be extended along the ridgeway to encompass Ketsby watermill and Calceby's ruined Norman church, or south to the fascinating village of Tetford. Otherwise continue past a rank of large beech trees before hurtling downhill into Ruckland, a farming settlement with the tiniest of churches. From here climb steeply past a youth hostel at Woody's Top, beyond which this road leads you between fields like massive rolling

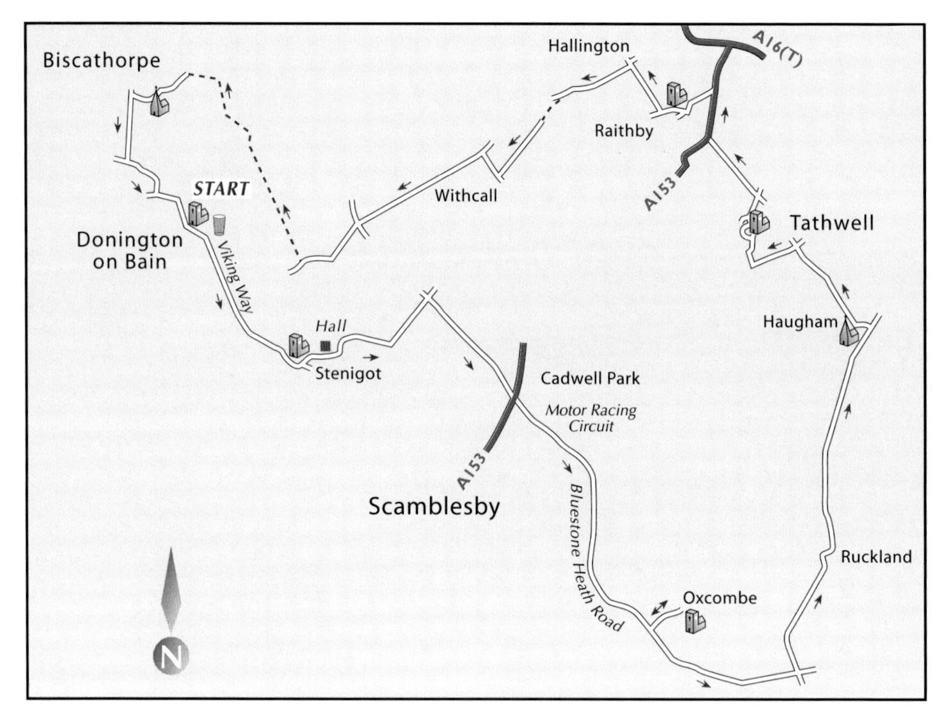

ocean waves, and reflect that if you believed them when they told you Lincolnshire was a flat county you have been the victim of a rather cruel joke.

Finally you reach a group of barns at Haugham – **turn L** (signed 'Tathwell') through the tiny village and pinpoint a narrow grassy lane on the left, twisting to All Saints', the second of the Nicholson churches. Back on the road continue for a mile and, having spotted a stark row of six Bronze Age round barrows on the Bully Hill skyline to your right, **turn L** into a lane opposite a pump gantry resembling a hangman's gallows. Now follow this lane into a farmyard, **turn R** past the final barn, and weave into the village of Tathwell. Look carefully for the Old Post Office, just past which you **turn L** into an even narrower lane leading you below the hidden church of Saint Vedast, around a sharp bend and to a T-junction. **Turn L** here and **turn R** at the next junction, where trees screen a charming lake on your left.

Ascend to another crossroads, **turn L** (signed 'Louth') and proceed high above a meandering stream to the main A153. Cross with caution and **turn R** (signed 'Louth') onto this road, but in less than ½ mile **turn L** (signed 'Raithby') at a converted barn. Now swoop down into Raithby, no more than a hamlet but unveiling, in a splendid

setting of ponds, gurgling streams and leafy trees, the next of the quartet of kindred churches – Saint Peter's. **Turn R** at the tall hedge of the Rectory (signed 'Hallington'), and then **turn L** (signed 'Withcall') when you reach the pleasant streamside farmstead of Hallington.

On your left in less than a mile locate Far Lodge, a lonely brick dwelling – **turn L** here to pass through an aluminium gate onto a good chalky track. Through a second gate at Keeper's Cottage the track upgrades to a metalled surface, and you enter the undisturbed settlement of Withcall. **Turn R** at the only junction amidst Withcall's prosperous looking halls and farms and **turn R** again at Home Farm to ascend sharply back to the Hallington road – **turn L** onto this. Continue to climb steadily towards a coronet of towering trees on the skyline, and through its central archway you once again meet the Bluestone Heath Road, this time crossing it and heading straight on towards the mighty pylon of one of the country's first radar stations at Stenigot.

Proceed past the pylon and, beyond a pair of brick houses on your right, look for a 'Public Bridleway' sign and **turn R** here onto a gravel track. Running parallel to the Bluestone Heath Road this trail offers splendid views over the Bain valley and of the curious toppled dishes of the adjacent radar station. It is also something of a challenge with an ever-changing terrain beneath you, but, apart from one road to cross and a gap in the hedgerow to identify above a combe, it makes a beeline north for 2 uninterrupted miles.

Eventually reaching an improved track **turn L**, then **turn L** again onto a cheery lane. Just visible above the trees is the tiny spire of the hidden church of Saint Helen's, completing the day's tour of Nicholson churches. **Turn L** at the next T-junction, then **turn L** at another (signed 'Stenigot'). Following signs for Donington-on-Bain, the road now brings you down to a bridge overlooking a picturesque white watermill building, and from here to your starting point in Donington.

THE NICHOLSON CHURCHES

Designed by the architect W.A. Nicholson of Louth in a cheerful Gothic Revival style, these four intriguing churches have a toy-like quality – look for buttresses, pinnacles, and elaborate openwork on the parapets. Constructed of rendered brick and varying in size, all are exquisitely situated. Raithby's square tower is the only one built around an original medieval shell, while Oxcombe and Biscathorpe are both capped by ornate octagonal lanterns, the latter also boasting a small spire. A bolder spire, an obvious miniature of Louth, tops Haugham, a rather neglected and spiritual site in a wilder setting.

10

From Alford to Burgh-le-Marsh

25 miles

Here's a ride linking two small market towns, each boasting one of the area's best restored working windmills. The scenery is a splendid mixture of wooded valleys and open farmland – some level, some not – all opening up vast panoramas across the coastal plain and the fens. The entire circuit is on first class road surfaces, and in addition offers you two optional walks to best see two stately halls, and a heroic tale of an American Indian princess.

Map: OS Landranger 122 Skegness & Horncastle (GR 455759).

Starting point: The North Market Place in Alford, which serves as a car park. There is an additional car park just off the South Market Place. Alford is situated 10 miles south-east of Louth, 3 miles along the A1104 from Ulceby Cross.

Refreshments: There are numerous excellent places to eat in Alford and Burgh-le-Marsh, including the tearoom at Hoyle's Mill. Between the two, inns at Willoughby, Orby, Skendleby and Ulceby (the Open Gate Inn) all cater for the hungry cyclist.

From the head of Alford's North Market Place proceed along East Street to pass the church and continue until you reach the five-sailed Hoyle's Mill on your left, overlooking a newly gravelled courtyard and a teashop. Now return and re-enter the North Market Place leading, naturally, through the South Market Place and into South Street, which carries you out of the town.

Three miles along this road, having passed Mawthorpe's former steam and transport museum, the road bends left to enter Willoughby. Follow the road around this lovely village, but venture briefly along a leafy lane from the Willoughby Arms to Saint Helena's church to investigate the links with the famous Elizabethan explorer and soldier, Captain John Smith. Born in Willoughby in 1579, Smith sailed to America, where he was saved from certain death by the Red Indian princess, Pocahontas. Return to the inn and **turn L** (signed 'Welton-le-Marsh'). Reaching Welton-le-Marsh, **turn L** (signed 'Habertoft') and follow this lane towards Habertoft, taking care to **turn R** at a bridge where the road ahead is signposted as a dead-end. This lane now winds

tortuously along the bank above Orby Beck until you reach a T-junction at which you **turn R** (signed 'Gunby') into Orby. **Turn L** (signed 'Burgh') at the Red Lion in Orby, and allow this road to guide you all the way into the centre of Burgh-le-Marsh.

Burgh-le-Marsh is more of a small town than a village, and as you **turn L** into the High Street, you pass the handsome old Market Place on your left and a warren of narrow streets and interesting brick buildings on your right, before reaching the turning point of the journey, Dobson's Mill. Return through Burgh-le-Marsh, this time keeping to the High Street as it twists past the mighty tower of the church and Cock Hill, so named because of its association with cockfighting but originally a pagan burial ground. At the converted tower of Burgh's other windmill **turn L** (signed 'Croft'), and then **turn R** (signed 'Bratoft') to enter Wildshed Lane and then a maze of lanes linked unfathomably to each other.

Passing a side road continue ahead (signed 'Bratoft'), but at the next junction **turn L** (virtually straight on) onto a lane merely labelled 'Unsuitable for HGVs'. After much twisting and turning you arrive at Bratoft's striking red brick church, at which you **turn L** (unsigned). Through Bratoft, **turn R** onto Brambleberry Lane, **turn L** at the T-junction (both signed 'Firsby'),

Alford

and proceed to another junction at the former Rising Sun inn – **turn R** here (signed 'Gunby'). Now spot the delightful thatched Whitegates Cottage on your right, an excellent specimen of traditional Lincolnshire mud and stud walling from the 1770s. **Turn R** after the cottage (signed 'Gunby') and, enjoying ever more prosperous surroundings, continue past Gunby Park to the main A158.

Turn L onto the A158 (signed 'Lincoln') and continue with care – during the summer months this road can be busy with holidaymakers heading to and from Skegness. Climb into

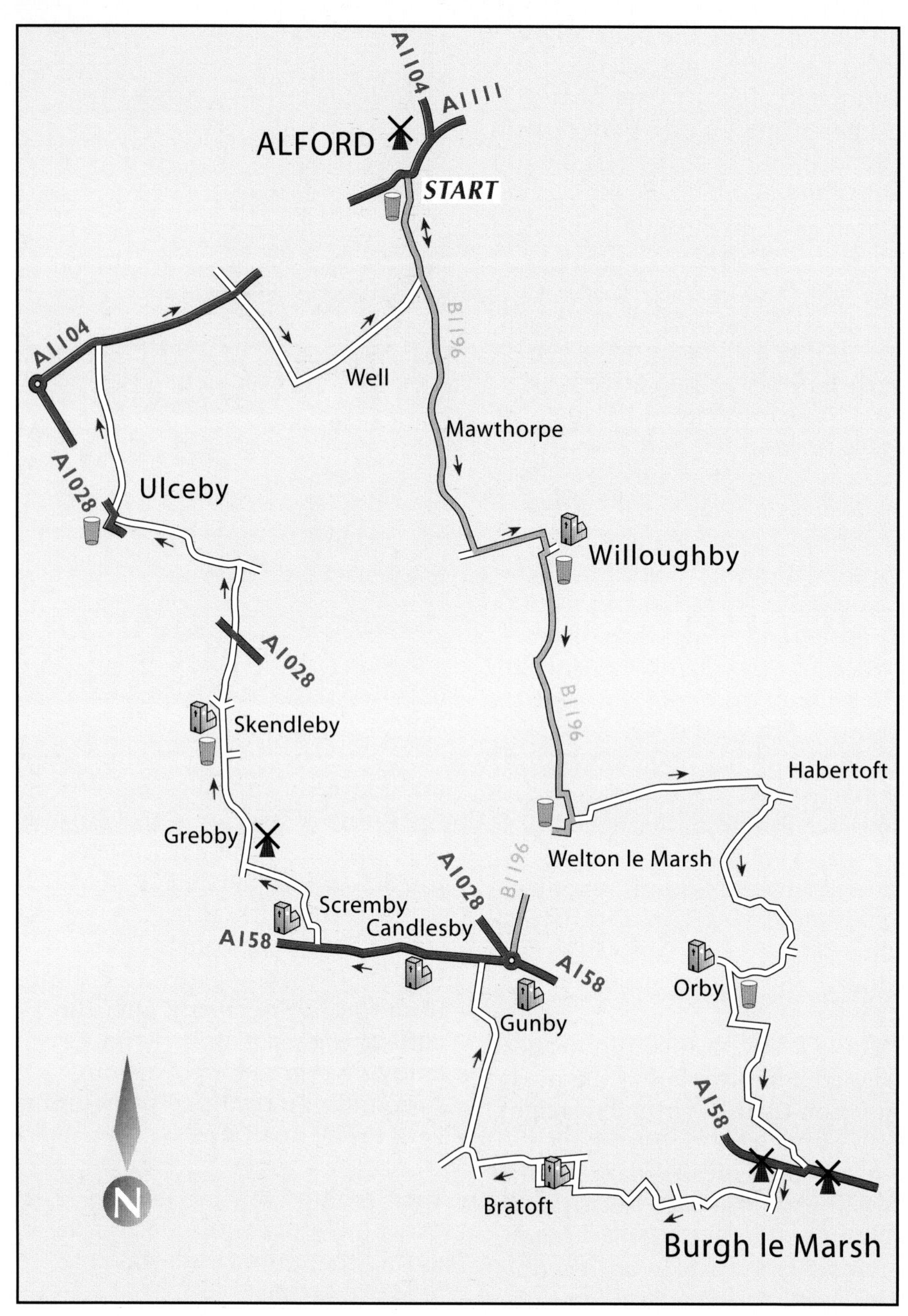
A1104
A1111
ALFORD
START
A1104
Well
B1196
Mawthorpe
A1028
Ulceby
Willoughby
A1028
B1196
Skendleby
Habertoft
Grebby
Welton le Marsh
B1196
A1028
Scremby
Candlesby
A158
A158
Orby
Gunby
A158
Bratoft
Burgh le Marsh
N

Candlesby and conduct a lap of Church Lane on your left before returning to the main road at the Royal Oak inn. Continue westwards and, where you spot a primrose-coloured house on the left flanked by two curious matching octagonal pavilions, you **turn R** (signed 'Scremby').

Now loins must be girded – you are about to trade in the level coastal marsh for the switchback heights of the Lincolnshire Wolds. Climb steeply past Scremby's Georgian church, before reaching a sylvan stretch of sloping parkland, studded with trees and leading you past a picturesque thatch beneath another converted windmill tower. **Turn R** at the T-junction (signed 'Skendleby') and proceed towards the long narrow village of that name. Skendleby is a picture – in addition to the ancient church and the imposing Hall, you will find an excellent country inn, the Blacksmith's Arms, and a 200 year old bowed shopfront of the Old Curiosity variety.

At a crossroads at the end of the village go straight ahead (signed 'Ulceby'), climb as far as a main road, and go straight ahead again onto an unsigned lane, which plummets down to the red pantile rooftops of the farming settlement of Skendleby Psalter. Here you **turn L** into a beautiful secluded valley, initially shaded by woods then opening out as it reaches a junction at the distinctive black and white Open Gate Inn. Here **turn R** onto the A1028 (signed 'Alford'), and, a few yards further on, **turn R** (signed 'Ulceby') to descend into Ulceby.

This road rises to a junction with another main road, onto which you **turn R** towards Alford. Through an area of wooded plantations the road begins to fall towards Alford, but you **turn R** where you see a sign for Well. Re-entering the dense woods this road spins left before descending through the attractive estate village of Well, with Well Vale Hall visible to your right. Continue to the next T-junction and **turn L** (signed 'Alford') onto the road that you will recognise from the beginning of the ride, with Alford's welcoming twin market places, inns and thatches just a few minutes away.

ALFORD AND BURGH-LE-MARSH

Here are two of the country's finest working windmills, both built by Sam Oxley of Alford in the early 19th century and both five-sailed. Hoyle's Mill in Alford has six floors, one more than Burgh's Dobson's Mill, but Burgh has the county's only left-handed sails – that is, they turn clockwise. Both towns are also proud of their parish churches. Look for a fine alabaster monument to the Christopher family in Alford's Saint Wilfrid's, and a colourful clockface on the tower of Saint Peter and Saint Paul's in Burgh, declaring a sinister warning; 'Watch and pray for ye know not when the time is'.

11

Horncastle, Tattershall and Old Bolingbroke

30 miles

The unspoilt market town of Horncastle is your gateway to a journey through sixteen hundred years of history and conflict, to the days when the Romans first made camp here. Two medieval castles of vastly differing fortunes, a network of Civil War connections and collections of irreplaceable aircraft from the last war transport you through the centuries to modern times. Disused railways and canals, along with once grandiose estates remind you that Lincolnshire's illustrious history is everywhere. The homeward leg is as hilly as the outward is flat, and an off-road section is encountered in each half.

Map: OS Landranger 122 Skegness & Horncastle (GR 258695).

Starting point: The Market Place in the centre of Horncastle, which is at the intersection of the A158 and the A153. There is parking in the square itself, but you may need to seek out public car parks next to the supermarkets behind the square – especially on market days.

Refreshments: Tearooms, inns, restaurants and shops abound in Horncastle, nor will you struggle for refreshment in Tattershall and Coningsby. There are also inns serving food at Kirkby-on-Bain, Mareham-le-Fen, Revesby and Old Bolingbroke, but you should note that beyond Bolingbroke no opportunities occur to replenish supplies.

Having thoroughly digested Horncastle's history and heritage (and allocated not too much time to scanning the countless antiques and bookshops – today's is a full schedule) exit the Market Place via the High Street to reach the busy junction known as the Bull Ring. **Turn R** here into South Street, cross the River Waring, go straight on at the traffic lights and proceed out of the town. After a mile, having passed White House Farm on your left, **turn R** into an unsigned road leading over the mere trickle of the Old River Bain and then the disused Horncastle Canal. Now locate a wooden bar gate on your left and **turn L** through it onto a narrow but firm track, the former bed of the Horncastle and Kirkstead Railway, indicated as a designated cycle track and also the Viking Way.

Initially confined, the trail opens out as the canal comes alongside –

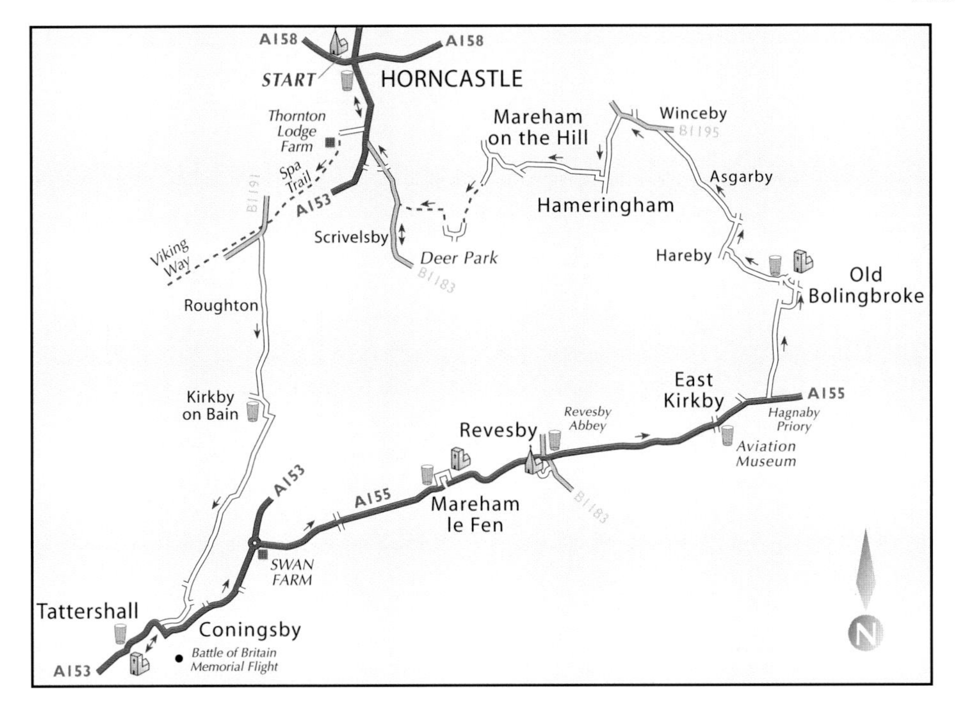

how different this picture of tranquillity and solitude is from the days when busy chugging narrowboats cast envious eyes up to the newly introduced steam trains thundering past and threatening their very existence. Pass under the impressive brick arch of Martin Bridge and continue as far as a picnic area. Here **turn L** onto a road doubling back towards Horncastle, but before the bridge **turn R** (signed 'Roughton') onto a pleasant undulating lane. Pass between Roughton's curious red brick church tower and pretty thatched white cottages and advance to Kirkby-on-Bain, an attractive leafy village of hidden bridges, mills and weirs along the canalised River Bain, also the willow-shaded Ebrington Arms.

Adhering to the main road proceed for 2½ miles through a surreal landscape of huge lagoons – flooded former sand and gravel pits. Where you espy the brick buttresses of a disused railway bridge **turn R** to pass between them into Hunter's Lane. Admire the Tudor herring-bone brickwork of Grange Farm on your right before you **turn L** at one T-junction and then **turn R** at another onto Tattershall High Street. At this point you will be stopped in your tracks by your first glimpse of the stupendous keep of Tattershall Castle ahead, and you will hasten towards this finest of medieval brick monuments – not only in Lincolnshire but in the whole of Britain.

It may be some time before you depart the castle precincts. An ascent of the mighty double-moated keep should be regarded as compulsory, and, as narrow stone steps spiral you up from floor to floor, views stretch out far across the fens. The parapet at the summit overlooks the Collegiate Church of the Holy Trinity – but you should not! This magnificent church of the Perpendicular period is beautifully light and airy, all glass and slender Gothic pillars, and neatly offset by a row of old low almshouses.

But at last you remount and begin to retrace your route, passing once again Tattershall's small but interesting Market Square, centred around an ancient buttercross. This time, however, continue over the River Bain into Coningsby – famous not only as home to the Battle of Britain Memorial Flight, but also for its horological oddity, the 17th century one-handed clockface of Saint Michael's church tower, at 16½ ft in diameter Europe's largest. Maintain your route along the A153 as far as a roundabout at Swan Farm, where you **turn R** (signed 'Spilsby') onto the A155, a delightful road leading you through woods and farmland to Mareham-le-Fen. Time permitting, explore the back lanes of Mareham behind the welcoming low white thatch of the Royal Oak, before continuing past the odd profile of Mareham's old windmill tower and on towards Revesby, a quite exceptional village.

Here, beyond a large farm on the right, **turn R** into an unsigned lane leading towards Saint Lawrence's church. Though impressive for a small estate village the tall spire is in fact no more medieval than the rest of the buildings around the spacious village green. Each building conforms to the estate style, including the Joseph Banks Almshouses, with their heavily latticed windows.

Exit the village green by the only other road, **turn L** at the T-junction, then **turn R** to rejoin the A153 (signed 'Spilsby'). Pass the remarkable wrought iron gates and railings which guard the avenue leading to Revesby Abbey, a stone built Elizabethan-style imposter – the abbey proper lay ½ mile south of the village. Progress towards East Kirkby, beyond which two bright red propellers mark the entrance to the Lincolnshire Aviation Heritage Centre, and a mile further on **turn L** (signed 'Old Bolingbroke') at Hagnaby Priory, whose fanciful 19th century arched gatehouse lies only a few yards off-route to the east.

With the hilly Wolds now closing in, you soon reach historic Old Bolingbroke. At Beech House on your left **turn R** (signed 'West Keal') and follow a winding lane alongside a stream until you spot the Old Post Office on the right – here **turn L** into an even narrower lane. Along this lane the ruins of Bolingbroke Castle may be entered,

more evocative than awesome – a little imagination is required to conjure up scenes from the castle's colourful history. Your lane continues past the Black Horse – the quintessential English country inn – and reaches a major junction at the Rose Garden, where you wheel to the left and, opposite The Lodge, **turn R** into an unsigned lane. Now you leave behind not only Old Bolingbroke but also the even terrain of the fenlands, as the constantly varying contours of the Wolds begin to examine you.

The tiny hilltop village of Hareby is soon reached, with its variety of delightful old buildings and a small neat church hidden in the trees beyond a Roman-style temple. At the junction near the duckpond **turn R** (signed 'Hagworthingham'), continue through a beech avenue to a crossroads at which you **turn L** (signed 'Asgarby'), then follow this long lane for 2 miles enjoying the views along the valleys below this plateau.

Reaching the T-junction at Winceby House **turn L** onto the B1195 (signed 'Horncastle') and pass the entrance to Snipe Dales Country Park on the right, an excellent spot for a moment's respite and a snack. Next on your right is Winceby Battlefield, scene of a bloody Civil War conflict in 1643, but you should **turn L** into the road signposted for Miningsby. A mile along here **turn R** (signed 'Hameringham') and weave through the small farming hamlet of that name. A mile further on **turn R** at a T-junction (signed 'Mareham-on-the-Hill') and just before Mareham's village sign locate Eastbeck Lane, an unsigned track leading down the hillside. **Turn L** here – although you may first wish to visit Mareham's tiny church, painted white and hidden behind handsome farm buildings.

Eastbeck Lane leads unerringly down to the wooded banks of Scrivelsby Beck, switching from a firm track to a green grassy lane midway. Beyond the beck you join a firmer chalky track meeting you from the left, climb the hill and curve slowly round towards a T-junction – **turn R** here onto a good metalled surface. Now entering the enchanting surroundings of the Scrivelsby estate you simply follow this lane past a farm (note the green clover-leaf shutters), over a ford in the middle of a gated pasture and through an area of open parkland.

The final gate opens onto a road – here you should **turn L** and advance through the deer park as far as the remarkable entrance to Scrivelsby Court. The mansion itself has largely vanished, but the arched stone gateway, surmounted by a crowned lion and embellished with shields, remains an arresting sight. Over your shoulder, sited inexplicably in the middle of a large open field, you will see the estate church, containing a wealth of memorials to the illustrious Dymokes of Scrivelsby Court. Now backtrack through the deer park and continue on the B1183 to a major junction with the A153. Carefully **turn R** here to be ushered back towards Horncastle, and the welcoming bustle of the Market Place.

HORNCASTLE

Horncastle has grown on the site of the Roman station of Banovallum – some fragments of the 4th century walls survive. The area played an important part in the English Civil War, and Saint Mary's church contains the tomb of Sir Ingram Hopton, who came so close to securing Cromwell's surrender to the Cavaliers at nearby Winceby, but who was himself finally slain and buried with honour at the request of the 'arch rebel'. Horncastle later gained renown for its Victorian horse fairs and is today popular as an antiques centre.

Tattershall Castle

TATTERSHALL CASTLE

Erected in 1455 by Ralph Cromwell, Treasurer to Henry VI, the six-storey brick keep was in fact built for show rather than defence. The benevolent Cromwell was also responsible for Tattershall's College and splendid Collegiate Church, the Bede Almshouses, the school and the construction of the Market Place. The not-so-benevolent Oliver Cromwell instigated the demise of the castle in the 17th century, and only Lord Curzon's intervention in 1910 rescued the derelict castle from demolition. The keep was restored to its former magnificence and subsequently presented to the nation.

The Lost Abbeys of the River Witham

27 miles

Sitting astride the Viking Way, Woodhall may be a splendid Edwardian spa town, but its relaxed resort atmosphere is not that of the ride proper. Six medieval monasteries once lined this short stretch of the River Witham – six have now almost completely vanished, leaving this peaceful landscape with an air of eerieness, a silence in total contrast to a time when the bells of these abbeys rang out in competition with each other. The route visits all six monastic sites, whose remains range from a few grassy ridges to huge crags of masonry reaching skywards. The wide River Witham itself and a series of bygone railway stations along its banks add to the mood of the ride, which, although flat throughout, encounters several challenging off-road sections.

Maps: OS Landranger 122 Skegness & Horncastle and 121 Lincoln and Newark-on-Trent (GR 193631).

Starting point: Royal Square in the town of Woodhall Spa, 6 miles south-west of Horncastle on the B1191. Roadside parking is available plus some small town centre parks, but Jubilee Park on Stixwould Road might be the best place to leave your car.

Refreshments: The area of Woodhall Spa and Kirkstead is well stocked with restaurants, tearooms, inns and shops – the village of Bardney likewise, but to a lesser degree. The Riverside Inn at Southrey is the only other refreshment opportunity along the route, but this may not be open at lunchtimes.

From Royal Square in the centre of Woodhall Spa cycle south along Tattershall Road, then **turn R** at a trim black and white inn called the Abbey Lodge. Where this new lane angles to the right a colossal finger of masonry, all that remains of Kirkstead Abbey, stands defiantly in the field to your left. Do not neglect to inspect this jagged pillar at close quarters because just beyond it is the tiny architectural gem of Saint Leonard's church, built outside the abbey gates in the early 13th century for lay worshippers, and remarkably well preserved.

Returning to the lane and continuing north-west, **turn L** when you reach Witham Road – the B1191. The vicinity of the bridge over the River Witham rewards a brief exploration. The new bridge is unremarkable, but to its left the old road passes the

Barlings Abbey

Railway Hotel before ending abruptly at the wide River Witham on the site of the former Woodhall Junction station.

Now retrace your route for ¼ mile and **turn L** into Mill Lane, which bends into Green Lane near the base of an old windmill. Green Lane leads you past a row of oaks to a crossroads near Petwood House, at which you **turn L** (signed 'Stixwould'), once again in entirely rural surroundings. Now simply follow this road through a series of right-angled bends, enjoying fine views over the nearby fields to the wooded horizon until, ½ mile later, you find yourself in Stixwould. **Turn L** at the first junction (signed 'Bucknall') then **turn R** (also signed 'Bucknall') at the second. Along Duckpool Lane the imposing whitewashed pile of Abbey Farm on your left stands where once stood the Cistercian priory, now entirely vanished.

Just beyond Duckpool Bridge **turn L** into the unsigned Holmes Road and at once **turn R** onto a chalky track leading to Willow Farm. This is very much a working farm and, although you will have no difficulty following the track through the farmyard, it is possible it may be a little, ahem, muddy. Soon enough, however, you emerge to continue along the track, but where this twists to the right beyond a small bridge you continue straight ahead, where an excellent grassy track guides you through three fields to the tarmac surface of Campney Lane. Continue straight ahead along the metalled lane opposite you which downgrades to a track through the gated yard of Abbey Warren Farm, before crossing Tupholme Beck and terminating at Ferry Road. Here **turn L** and enter the isolated village of Southrey, which, like Kirkstead, comes to a halt at the eerie old railway station, huge gaunt concrete name boards still prominent and forlorn jetties watching the deep, broad Witham flowing by.

Returning along Ferry Road you will be uplifted by a visit to the tiny white church on your right, erected at the turn of the century by the parishioners themselves and

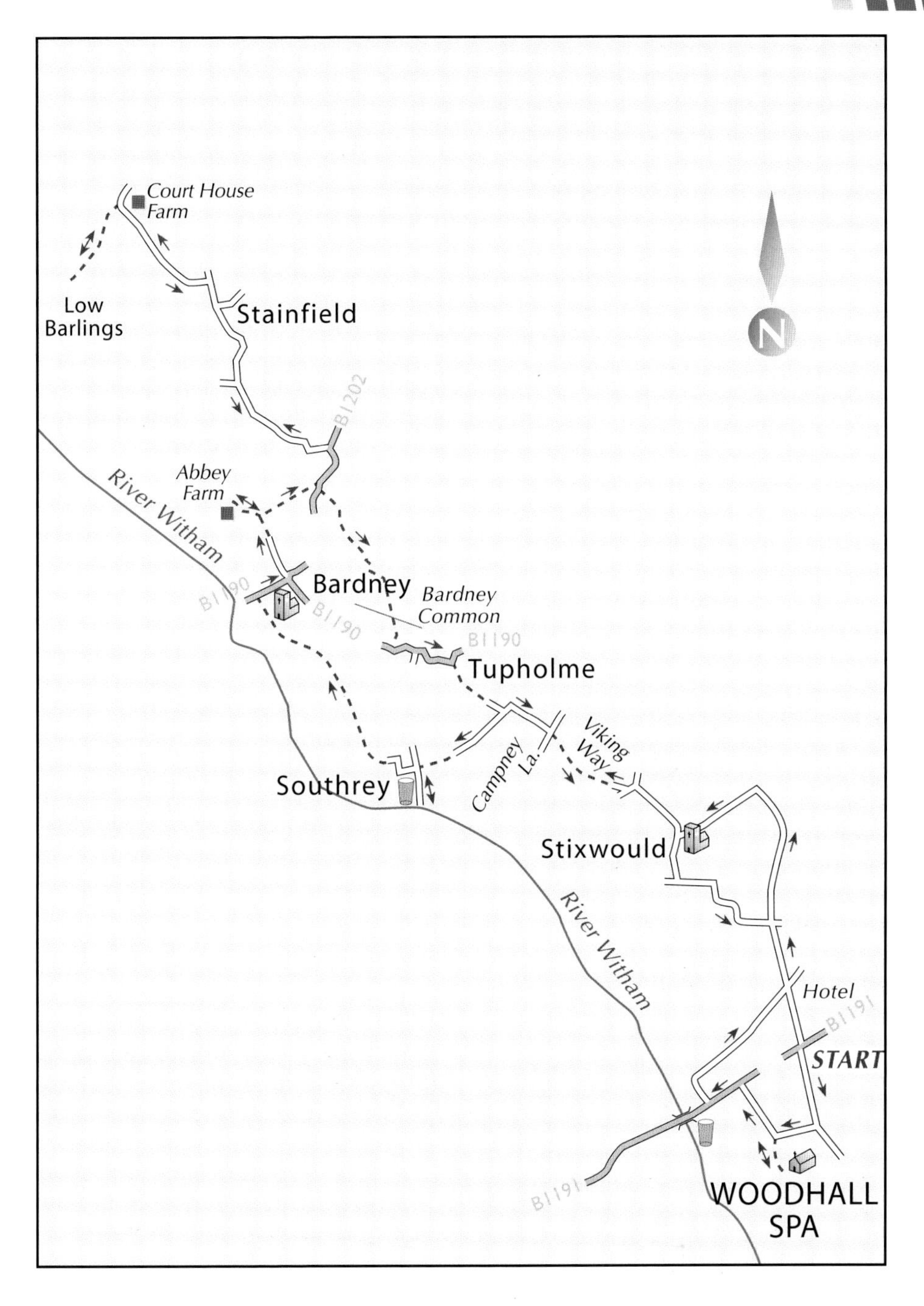
Court House Farm
Low Barlings
Stainfield
B1202
Abbey Farm
River Witham
Bardney
Bardney Common
B1190
B1190
B1190
Tupholme
Southrey
Campney La.
Viking Way
Stixwould
River Witham
Hotel
B1191
START
B1191
WOODHALL SPA
N

resembling a settlers' chapel from a New England outpost. **Turn L** just past here into High Thorpe, which leads you past a fine specimen of a mud-and-stud thatch to Poplar Farm. **Turn L** again here where Westfield Road, at first a good track, leads you between open fields to the vast Southrey Wood. Follow this track faithfully along the west edge of the wood, at the end of which the way appears to veer to the right near a raised fuel drum. You, however, strike left onto a lesser path, keeping the distinctive tall cylinders of the apparently doomed sugar beet factory on your left – eventually the path rises and you enter the historic village of Bardney.

By now you know the drill – down to the Witham, where the disused railway and the abandoned station follow the previously set pattern. Now return to the heart of the village, which is full of intriguing details, before seeking out Abbey Road opposite an inn called Bards. Here **turn L** and allow this lane to guide you out of the village to Abbey Farm, beyond whose yard lie the evocative remains of Bardney Abbey itself, beautifully situated but now little more than a series of turf outlines.

Cycle back to the curious red brick water tower near the farm and **turn L** onto the public bridleway to its left, leading you past King's Hill to a road onto which you **turn L**. At a sharp bend **turn L** again (signed 'Short Ferry') to cross a disused railway bridge. A mile further on **turn R** (signed 'Stainfield') to keep Stainfield Wood on your right. Reaching a lane signed 'Kingsthorpe' **turn R** to visit the hamlet of Stainfield, not considered one of the route's main abbey sites but still displaying some earthworks and fish ponds from the vanished Benedictine priory. The visit to this intriguing cluster of buildings should not be omitted before you return to the main road and continue on your way.

After another mile you arrive at Court House Farm on your right, opposite which a chalky track leads into the fields. Your true route, however, is to **turn L** through the green gates 100 yards away, where a grassy bridleway angles across a pasture to join the chalk track, and you continue along it to its terminus. From here your destination looms large ahead of you, the imposing fragment of the Premonstratensian abbey at Barlings. Excellent information boards explain the history and erstwhile grandeur of the site.

Suitably impressed, now about turn and retrace your route all the way to the bridleway near to King's Hill. This time, instead of turning towards Bardney Abbey, follow the road for a few more yards before you **turn L** onto a grassy bridleway leading towards Scotgrove Wood. This green strip traces the edge of the wood for ½ mile, before leading you through two gates and a

farmyard to a busy road. Cross and continue along another bridleway whose surface is firmer and whose views around Bardney Common are exceptional. Only the last few yards present any difficulty, and, reaching Horncastle Road, you **turn L** with Southrey Wood once again on your right.

Half a mile further **turn R** where a signed bridleway leads to the last of the day's ecclesiastical edifices – Tupholme Abbey. Here an entire wall of the refectory survives, surrounded by more information boards and a flock of very inquisitive Soay sheep. Beyond the abbey the masonry-strewn track leads past an old brick farm building before emerging onto a narrow rural lane – **turn L** here. Recognising the lane from the earlier part of your journey, follow the route in reverse (via that farmyard!) until you are back in the village of Stixwould.

To vary the return journey **turn R** (virtually straight on), signed 'Stixwould Station', at Stixwould's old school building, **turn L** at the unsigned junction near a handsome L-shaped barn, and **turn R** to rejoin the main road. From here a few zigzags guide you onto the home straight back into Woodhall Spa, this time returning past the imposing Petwood House Hotel, between the charming Jubilee Park and the woods containing the former spa buildings and back to your starting point in Royal Square.

THE ABBEYS OF THE WITHAM VALLEY

Of the hundred or more medieval religious houses in Lincolnshire the greatest concentration was along the banks of the River Witham, which provided transport for the wool upon which the wealth of these abbeys was based. However, far more spectacular than their rise was their collapse following the Dissolution of the Monasteries in 1536, which upheaval sparked the Lincolnshire Rising. This rebellion was swiftly quashed, but incurred greater wrath upon the monasteries concerned than elsewhere, in an effort to ensure that there would be no rekindling of unrest in the future.

Originally founded in the 7th century by King Ethelred – whose body lies in the nearby barrow of King's Hill – Bardney is the oldest and most notable of these abbeys. When the bones of the martyr Saint Oswald were brought here and refused admission to the abbey it took a divine message in the form of a startling pillar of light to persuade the monks to open the doors and permit entry, giving rise to the Bardney tradition of leaving doors open, and the question 'Do you come from Bardney?' asked of those who habitually neglect to close doors! The ruins of the abbey were excavated and thoroughly studied in 1909 but then covered over again to protect them. A fine model of the abbey at its height can be seen in the village church.

Both Barlings and Kirkstead Abbeys exhibit single crags of stonework set in their surrounding earthworks, while the arches of Tupholme Abbey's refectory wall embrace a beautiful recessed Reader's Pulpit, from which a monk would read gospels while the others ate in silence. Earthworks also indicate the position of Stainfield Priory, but of Stixwould few traces remain.

13
The Car Dyke

20 miles

This ride focuses on a beautiful stretch of the Car Dyke, a Roman waterway separating the gentle slopes of the Lincoln Heath from the wide plain through which the River Witham flows towards endless fenlands. Your approach and return from the Dyke is via a string of intriguing villages, well stocked with warm stone buildings. The area is a natural treasure chest of woodland plant and wildlife, and a number of fine modern sculptures punctuate the route. Your rewards are well earned as much of the central part of the journey is off-road, though nowhere difficult, and all gradients are shallow.

Map: OS Landranger 121 Lincoln & Newark-on-Trent (GR 069615).

Starting point: The village of Metheringham, situated just east of the B1188 midway between Lincoln and Sleaford. Two signed roads lead into the village, where roadside parking is not a problem. In addition Metheringham is served by a railway linking Lincoln and Sleaford.

Refreshments: All villages en route feature good inns, the only exceptions being Nocton, Kirkby Green and Blankney, while the best is the Penny Farthing in Timberland. But note that the long stretch along the Dyke itself, though pleasant and peaceful, is barren of refreshment opportunities.

Metheringham is large for a village – and expanding still – but at its heart you will find several fine old houses and inns. The oldest structure is the 14th century village cross, whose base and shaft were retired to a roadside niche when superseded by their modern replacement. From this cross proceed north along High Street and go straight ahead at the junction with Lincoln Road (signed 'Dunston'). In less than a mile you reach the village of Dunston, where you **turn R** into Front Street just before a small brook goes under the road – having first crossed this bridge to inspect the wooden sculpture of King George III and Saint Peter's church.

Front Street becomes Middle Street and winds past the inviting Red Lion inn. Next **turn R** into Backs Lane, pass the school and locate a narrow tarmac bridleway, onto which you also **turn R**. After an enjoyable mile along here you emerge in the stone estate village of Nocton. The high steeple of All Saints' crowns one of Lincolnshire's most distinguished churches, built

Scopwick

of warm Ancaster stone. Sir George Gilbert Scott was commissioned to build the church as an extravagant monument to the Earl of Ripon (alias 'Prosperity Robinson'), a spectacularly incompetent Prime Minister, but still a much loved husband.

Returning from the church **turn R** at the post office (signed 'Bardney') and continue through the leafy streets of Nocton village, heading north towards Potterhanworth – named, simply enough, from its medieval origins as a major earthenware centre. The village's approach is heralded by an extraordinary Edwardian water tower, whose decorative brick base is surmounted by a huge green iron tank, itself capped by an overhanging slate roof. Remain faithful to the road carrying you out of the village until, 1½ miles later, it terminates at a major junction opposite the Plough Inn. **Turn R** here and immediately **turn R** again onto a grassy public bridleway.

You are now following the course of the Car Dyke itself, and you will soon become familiar with the format. To the right the far bank of the Dyke slopes upwards through ancient woodlands, rich in wildlife and sheltering a wide range of

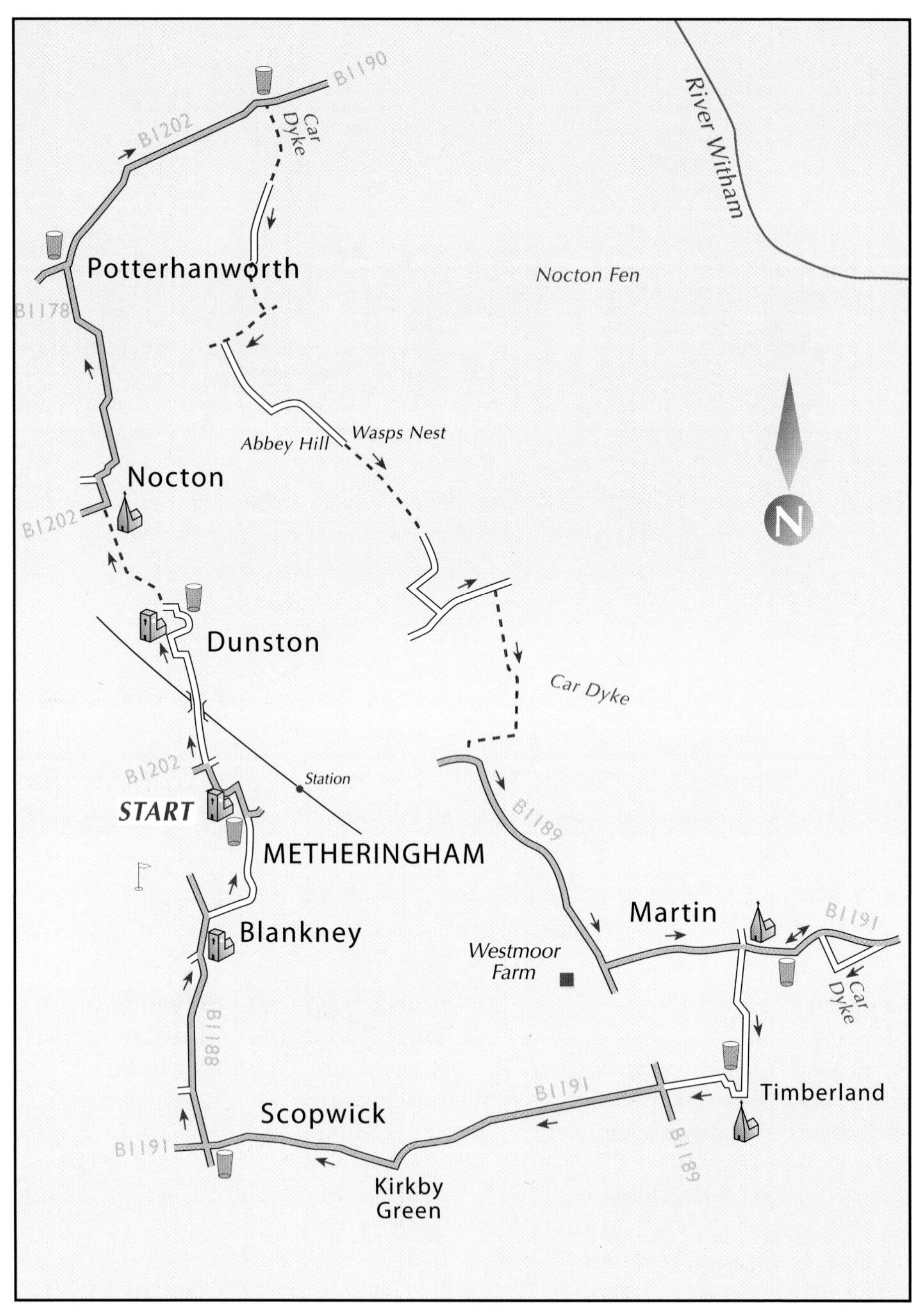

B1190
Car Dyke
B1202
River Witham
Potterhanworth
Nocton Fen
B1178
Abbey Hill
Wasps Nest
Nocton
B1202
N
Dunston
Car Dyke
B1202
Station
START
METHERINGHAM
Martin
B1191
Blankney
Westmoor Farm
Car Dyke
B1188
B1191
Timberland
Scopwick
B1191
B1189
Kirkby Green
B1189

birdlife, including nightingales and tawny owls. To the left open views stretch across the vast arable fenlands to the Lincolnshire Wolds and Bardney. Soon the grassy track joins a metalled lane for a while, but before this crosses a railed bridge you should **turn L** onto the bridleway and continue alongside the Dyke, before angling left towards a junction at a Lincolnshire Cycle Trail sign. **Turn R** here, cross the Dyke and ascend the dirt track between the woods, which soon arrives at a lane onto which you **turn L**.

This delightful lane descends into a basin from which it escapes by veering to cross and rejoin the Dyke, which you follow to the farming hamlet of Wasps Nest, imaginatively named, idyllically situated. Around the wooded hill to your right lie the earthworks of the 12th century Nocton Park Priory. The road crooks left at Wasps Nest to cross Nocton Fen, but you should continue straight ahead through the silver gates onto an excellent gravel track signed as a 'Permissive Cycle Path', keeping the Dyke on your right.

Meeting a surfaced lane at a picnic area, **turn R** and circle the corner of the wood. **Turn L** at a white wooden cottage then **turn L** again at the T-junction (both signed 'Metheringham Fen'). In less than ½ mile carefully locate an unsigned bridleway at a yellow single-bar gate and **turn R** onto this. The firm track meets a broader one onto which you **turn R**, cross the Dyke once more and ascend to pass the handsome brick range of Barff Farm. After another mile and two more right angles your track reaches the somewhat busier B1189, onto which you **turn L** and proceed with due care for 1½ miles, noting the disused concrete runways of Metheringham Airfield and the 106 Squadron Memorial on your left.

Arriving at the B1191 **turn L** (signed 'Martin'). At this point the Metheringham Airfield Visitor Centre is situated in the opposite direction. Descend the High Street in Martin, a neat brick-built village, cross the bridge at the foot of the hill and **turn R** to follow a final section of the Car Dyke. Where a gate bars your way **turn L**, pass a corrugated iron barn, **turn L** again to rejoin the road and return to the bridge. Bidding farewell to the Dyke climb back through Martin and **turn L** into Timberland Road at the school (signed 'Timberland'). The Stables in Martin and Timberland's Methodist chapel possess a surprising link in that both have been converted to thriving art and craft galleries.

Timberland's Church Street culminates in Saint Andrew's sturdy stone church tower – about turn here and return to the Tudor-style schoolhouse, but this time **turn L** into West Street. Twist this way and that, pass (if you can!) the

ivy-clad Penny Farthing inn, and proceed along Station Road which leads you back to the B1189. Cross carefully and follow the straight road ahead of you to Kirkby Green, notable not so much for the little church from which it takes its name as for a series of former watermill buildings strung along the stream which flows through the fields to your left, and which you rejoin when you enter the village of Scopwick.

Scopwick portrays a most enchanting picture, where bridges cross the stream running between parallel lanes flanked by stone cottages. At the Royal Oak, a delightful ivy-covered stone-built inn, the village meets the busy B1188. **Turn R** (signed 'Lincoln') and progress carefully for a mile to arrive at a fitting finale to the ride – the model estate village of Blankney, laid out in the 1830s by W. A. Nicholson, the architect responsible for the four churches along the Bluestone Heath Road ride (Route 9). Nowadays the local golf club has seemingly taken the pick of the ornate Tudor-style stone buildings. **Turn R** (signed 'Blankney') at the central crossroads and continue past the most perfectly sited cricket green and leave the village. Arcing around a wooded bend allow Drury Street to guide you into Metheringham, passing on your left the splendid Vicarage on your way back to the ancient village cross.

THE CAR DYKE

What is the Car Dyke? Certainly a waterway constructed by the Romans, and the rather romantic notion of trading vessels plying back and forth along this canal remained unchallenged until the 1970s. Research then concluded that the Dyke was actually a catchwater drain stretching for 76 miles from the Witham near Lincoln south to the River Nene, part of a complex system enabling the reclamation of this area of fenland from the sea. The geography of the area is interesting. Each elongated parish, though only a mile wide, has a length of some 10 miles – thus each village owns an area of heathland, a wooded slope or 'barff' and an arable fenland stretch.

DUNSTON PILLAR AND KING GEORGE III

Simon Todd's sculpture of King George III in Dunston, carved from a local ash tree, mirrors the stone statue which once looked across these heathlands from the top of the lofty Dunston Pillar, lying 3 miles to the west and originally constructed as a land lighthouse to guide 18th century travellers across these notorious parts. George's statue has since been proudly remounted in the grounds of Lincoln Castle but the Pillar was deemed a danger to low-flying aircraft and only the lower portion now remains. Simon's version of George was inspired by the Pillar, and is one of a series of contemporary wooden sculptures along and around the Car Dyke area.

14

Navenby: Along the Lincoln Cliff

23 miles

Sandwiched between two historic Roman roads – Ermine Street and the Fosse Way – this route links two chains of entirely different settlements. Along the edge of the escarpment known as the Lincoln Cliff run a series of picturesque stone-built villages, while westwards across the valley of the River Witham imposing red brick buildings dominate. In these villages you will see some of the land's most impressive parish churches, especially those capped by elegant stone spires. The whole journey is on fine road surfaces, but the Cliff section involves several steep climbs. The area is richly endowed with contemporary sculptures and mosaics – look out for these as you follow the route.

Map: OS Landranger 121 Lincoln & Newark-on-Trent (GR 988577).

Starting point: The village of Navenby can be found 8 miles south of Lincoln on the A607. Park either on the High Street or in one of several side roads. Railway stations at North Hykeham and Swinderby are just 3 miles off-route.

Refreshments: Few of the villages do not contain a decent inn or a shop. Particularly worth a visit are the Bell in Coleby, Aubourn's Royal Oak and the Generous Briton in Brant Broughton. Good tearooms are also available in Navenby and Fulbeck.

Head north along Navenby's broad High Street – remain alert as this road linking Grantham and Lincoln can be busy. Shortly you arrive at Boothby Graffoe's tall, neat church tower. **Turn L** here to execute a circuit of the village's old stone houses before returning to the main road, onto which you **turn L**. A stretch of cycle path leads you to the next stone village, that of Coleby, worthy of a more thorough exploration. **Turn L** into Dovecote Lane (signed 'Coleby') and, at Blind Lane, go straight ahead, keeping a weathered stone wall on your right and the Tempest Arms on your left. The church tower ahead of you dates from before the Norman Conquest, although the crocketed spire was not added until the 15th century. A hidden inn called the Bell lies beyond the church, but you **turn R** into Rectory Road which leads you back to the main A607 – **turn L**.

Harmston is your next destination and the place where, in 1904, a meeting of farmers at the Harmston Hall agricultural show led to the formation of the

Coleby

National Farmers Union. **Turn L** into Church Lane (signed 'Harmston') and **turn R** at the church into High Street. In the churchyard lies John Willson who erected the stone statue of George III atop the nearby Dunston Pillar (2½ miles to the east), from which he fell to his death in 1810. His gravestone bears a relief carving of the Pillar and the inscription:

> He who erected the noble King
> Here laid low by Death's sharp sting.

Turn L at the Thorold Arms into Blacksmith's Lane. Stunning views now extend over the valleys of the Rivers Brant and Witham, and you **turn R** at a junction with a superior road to speed down the hillside towards this plain. Continue for 3 miles until you reach Aubourn – **turn L** (virtually straight on) at the only junction along the way (signed 'Aubourn'). Aubourn Hall on your right is a 16th century country house set in lush gardens and hidden to its right is the restored chancel of the medieval church. The village conducts you around a one-way system, and a lap of the entire village is recommended to avoid missing the excellent Royal Oak. Following signs for Haddington, continue in your original direction and **turn R** (also signed 'Haddington') at another

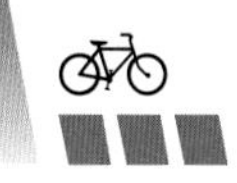

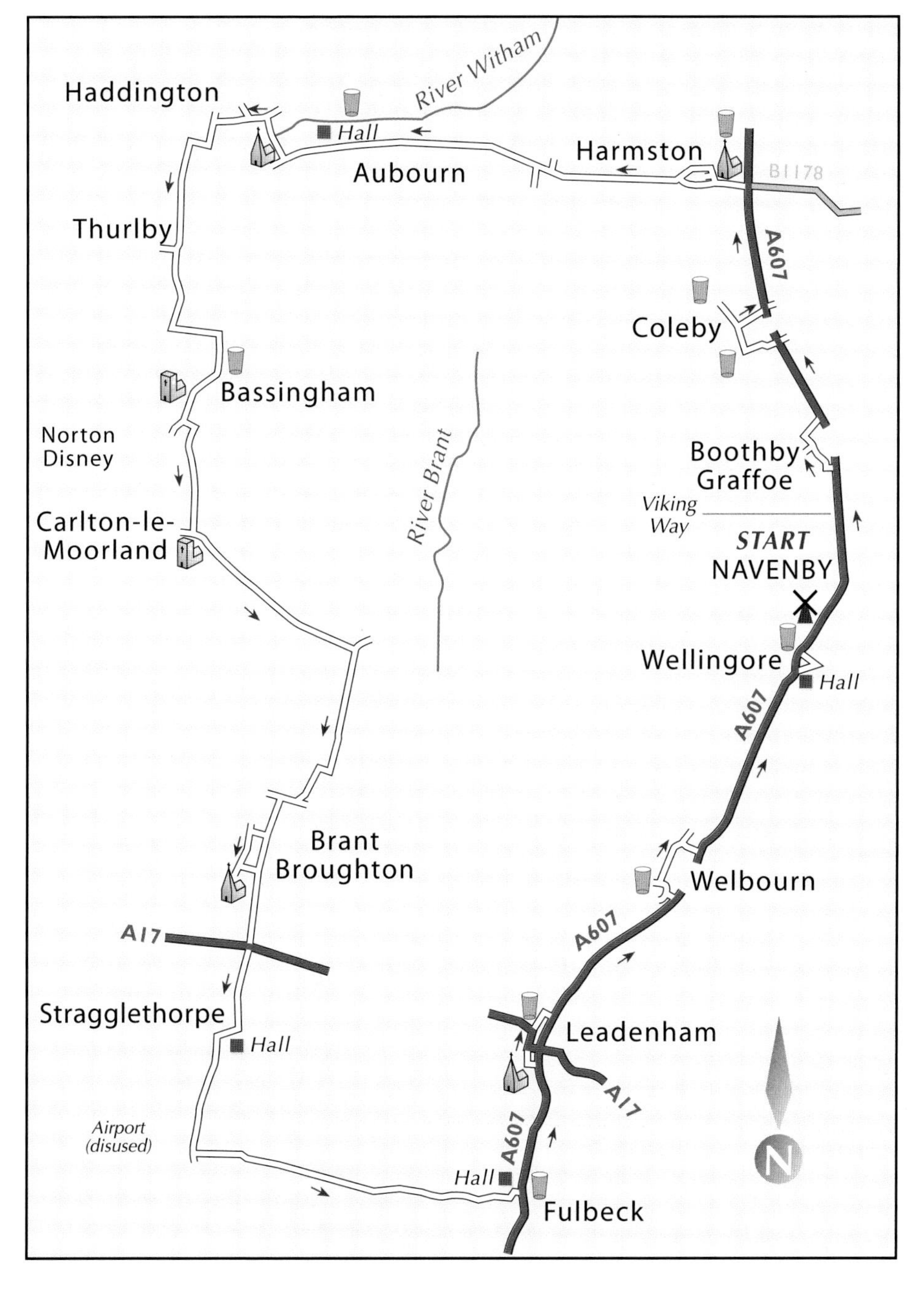
River Witham
Haddington
Hall
Aubourn
Harmston
B1178
Thurlby
A607
Coleby
Bassingham
Norton
Disney
River Brant
Boothby
Graffoe
Viking
Way
START
NAVENBY
Carlton-le-
Moorland
Wellingore
Hall
A607
Brant
Broughton
Welbourn
A17
A607
Stragglethorpe
Hall
Leadenham
A17
Airport
(disused)
A607
Hall
Fulbeck
N

ecclesiastical fragment, the Victorian tower of Saint Peter's.

Having crossed the River Witham **turn L** (signed 'Haddington') and **turn L** again into the narrow Dovecote Lane where you see a modern sculpture with copper tablets depicting local wildlife, set in a wooden frame. Pass the stone-built dovecote on your left, all that remains above ground of the moated site of Haddington Hall. **Turn L** (signed 'Thurlby') at the T-junction to follow the lane around the medieval site and on to Thurlby. Here **turn L** (signed 'Bassingham') before crossing the Witham once more, beyond a sharp bend. **Turn R** (signed 'Carlton-le-Moorland') into Croft Lane which soon becomes the High Street running through Bassingham, a village of handsome brick houses and a network of narrow lanes. Behind the Wesleyan chapel the parish council have created a Heritage Room, where you may delve into the village's fascinating history. It is an admirable set-up and the countryside would be far richer were more villages to follow Bassingham's example and establish similar centres.

Pass the wooden carving of the Bassingham Bull on your left and the church of Saint Michael and All Angels on your right, **turn L** into White's Road, **turn R** at the T-junction (both signed 'Carlton-le-Moorland') and proceed into the village of that name. In Carlton **turn L** at the crossroads into Broughton Road, unless you wish to explore the village itself – and, yes, the neighbouring village of Norton Disney was once governed by the Disney family of which the creator of Mickey and Donald was a descendant. In a mile Broughton Road brings you to a wider road – here **turn R** (signed 'Brant Broughton'). In the opposite direction are situated the round stone towers of Somerton Castle, now incorporated into a farm and only glimpsed with difficulty through the trees.

From the moment you enter Brant Broughton you are aware that this is a special place, its wide main street lined with imposing houses, mainly brick-built and too numerous to list. But it is the magnificent steeple, soaring to a height of almost 200 ft, from which you will be unable to tear your gaze. The interior of Saint Helen's is even more awe-inspiring and is that rare thing, a Victorian restoration which sympathetically amplifies the medieval glories already in place.

Beyond Brant Broughton carefully **turn R** onto the busy A17 (signed 'Newark') and immediately **turn L** into a lane leading towards Stragglethorpe, passing on your right the yard of Brant House Farm, in which sits a tiny Saxon chapel of charming simplicity. Twist past the Elizabethan Stragglethorpe Hall (famous for its vineyards) and

through the village, advance another mile and **turn L** (signed 'Fulbeck') just past a cluster of farms.

Two miles along this lane you ascend into Fulbeck and complete the transition back from brick to stone. Scott's Hill leads you into High Street and, at the Hare and Hounds, you **turn R** into Rectory Lane, emerging once more onto the A607 at the Manor Stables, where a group of craft workshops surround a first-class teashop. There is much to see in Fulbeck and you will find a lengthy exploration rewarding. Of particular note are the elegant pinnacled tower of Saint Nicholas' church and Fulbeck Hall itself, rebuilt by the Fane family in 1733 following a fire, and commandeered in 1944 as the First Airborne Division's HQ at the time of the fateful Arnhem mission.

Turn L to pass inn, church and Hall in succession and proceed to Leadenham, lured by another lofty spire. Past the church **turn L** into Rectory Lane, but then bear right to pass a huge rusticated stone arch, the gateway to Leadenham House. At the George Hotel **turn R** to continue between the stone houses along the High Street, which finally turns to the right and rejoins Cliff Road, onto which you **turn L**, continuing along the A607 for just over a mile. At a sign for Welbourn **turn L** and descend Hall Lane into the village. At the foot of the hill follow the road to the right into High Street, which becomes Moat Lane as it rounds the overgrown mound where once stood the stone walls of the 12th century castle. The curious taper of the church spire to your left is known architecturally as 'entasis' but has led to the steeple being likened to a sugarloaf, a rocketship and even a half-cucumber!

Climb all the way back to Cliff Road, **turn L** and proceed to the final village of your outing, Wellingore. **Turn R** at the church into Hall Street to examine the finery of Wellingore Hall, then **turn L** into High Street, passing two inns as you wind back to Cliff Road for the last time. **Turn R** and, from here, Wellingore blends almost unnoticeably into Navenby, and the completion of your journey.

NAVENBY

Sitting astride both the Roman Ermine Street and the Viking Way, Navenby was once a thriving, self-sufficient market town. Nowadays the market, the fairs and the craftsmen have vanished, leaving a wide High Street lined with many listed stone buildings. But behind these stone fronts can be found one red brick building of particular interest. Mrs Smith's Cottage in East Road was built 200 years ago and occupied by Hilda Smith from the 1920s until 1994, when she was 102! She managed to resist 20th century change for the whole of that time, even retaining the wooden ladder accessing the first floor bedrooms. This remarkable survival is now open to the public.

15
The Spires and Steeples of Sleaford

30 miles

Lincolnshire's greatest glory is its wealth of medieval churches and the soaring spires around Sleaford and North Kesteven are not matched throughout the land. The trinity of Sleaford, Heckington and Ewerby consists of near-perfect examples of Decorated Gothic architecture and forms the basis of this whole-day outing. These spires dominate the wide open views as you travel across fens and hills, through market towns and unspoilt countryside. Add windmills and watermills, ancient villages and a breathtaking piece of industrial archaeology, and you have a full and rewarding itinerary indeed.

Maps: OS Landranger 130 Grantham and 121 Lincoln & Newark-on-Trent (GR 068458).

Starting point: The station at the south end of Southgate in the town of Sleaford. Sleaford itself is easily found where the A15 and the A17 meet. There is some parking here as well as car parks in the town and roadside parking on the other side of the railway lines. Needless to say this spot is supported by a good train service.

Refreshments: You will find plenty of restaurants, inns and shops around Sleaford – but thankfully no fast food outlets as yet. Ruskington and Heckington also offer numerous refreshment opportunities, while excellent inns at Ewerby, Aswarby, Oasby and Silk Willoughby all serve food.

Before you even set off on the ride proper you are side-tracked to behold one of the country's most awesome pieces of industrial architecture. At the end of the Station Approach **turn R**, cross the tracks, and then **turn L** into Mareham Lane. In a few hundred yards locate a set of arched stone pillars and iron gates on your left and through these you approach the staggering ruins of the Bass Maltings. A row of eight brick pavilions, each of which would itself be a remarkable monument, are linked to each other and focused upon a huge square central tower. Though dilapidated, the brickwork, the ornate iron mouldings, the overhanging canopies and the sheer scale of these warehouses get the day off to a rousing start.

Retrace your route back over the railway, but this time continue through the centre of Sleaford and past the stone monument to Henry

St Andrew's church, Heckington

Handley, noting the contemporary street furniture and sculpture nearby. **Turn R** into Eastgate and pass the cheerful little Market Place, sheltered by the dramatic west front and spire of Saint Denys' church. Continue past the Carre Almshouses and, making use of the cycle lane which begins a little further on, proceed as far as Cogglesford Mill on your right. Having thoroughly inspected the quaint old brick mill, maintain your original route until you cross a hump-backed railway bridge and arrive at a large roundabout. Carefully negotiate this (dismount if necessary) and again continue ahead on the A153 (signed 'Horncastle'), once more joining a shared cycle lane.

After a mile **turn L** onto the lesser B1188 (signed 'Ruskington'), which leads you into the village of Ruskington, with seemingly an inn on every corner. At the Black Bull continue ahead into Church Street, then **turn R** into the High Street, where the Beck runs between the two halves of the road. At the Red Lion **turn R** into Chestnut Street, then **turn L** at a T-junction into Station Road. Past the station and over the bridge, twist right then left until a small lane continues in front of you where the road bends right (the sign reads 'Road used as a

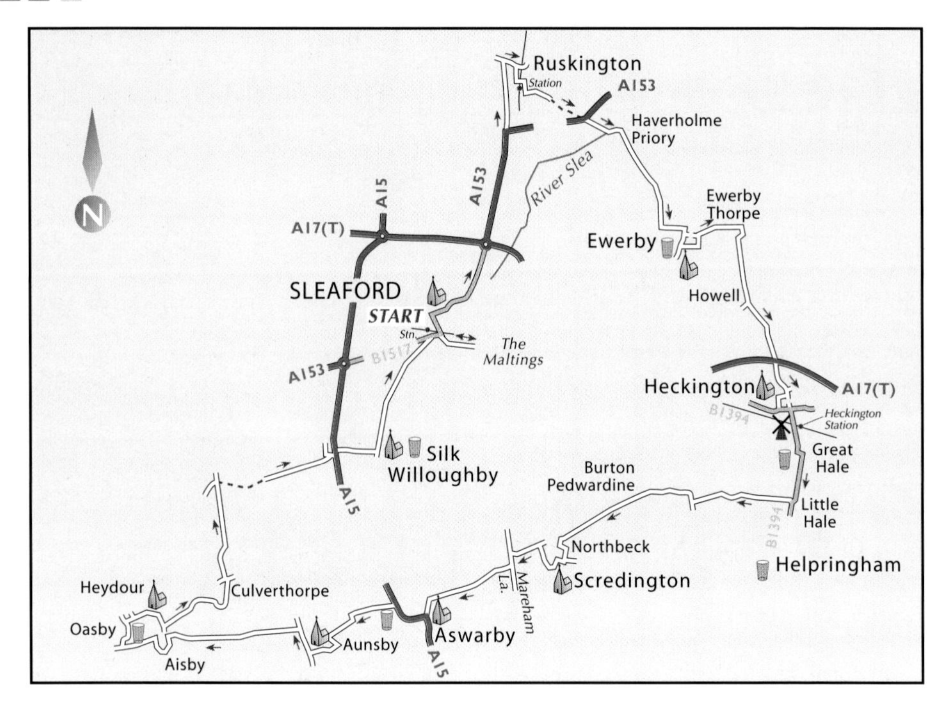

public path'). A few yards along here a clear grassy byway shoots off the track and you **turn R** to follow this between the fields, to emerge at a busy main road. Follow the obvious lane (signed 'Ewerby') on the other side of this road to a graceful stone bridge spanning the beautiful River Slea, beyond which a small car park will offer you the best views of the gaunt romantic ruins of Haverholme Priory.

A mile further on this lane turns left then right to enter Ewerby, a village which features a compendium of building styles. **Turn L** just past the church onto a narrow lane that twists this way and that before emerging onto an open road where you **turn R**.

Beyond the hamlet of Ewerby Thorpe **turn R** (signed 'Howell'). The numerous spires and steeples which dominate the day's route are in contrast to the tiny crooked nave of the church in Howell. As well as these spires, the medieval tower in South Kyme and the 'Stump' of Saint Botolph's in Boston can be seen on the horizon. When this long lane reaches a stable and bends left to join the A17, dismount and walk through a dim tunnel under the road. The lane in which you find yourself leads you into the centre of Heckington, a treasure chest of fascinating old buildings. Cameron Street passes Saint Andrew's church, and at Church Street you **turn L**. Past the village green you **turn L**

again into High Street, and then **turn R** into Station Road at the Royal Oak. After the Pearoom Gallery and the station on your left, a level crossing still operated by a real person, and the eight-sailed windmill on your right, continue through Great Hale towards Little Hale.

Just before Little Hale **turn R** onto a quiet winding lane (signed 'Burton'). Along this lane views right and left to the spires of Heckington and Helpringham mirror each other – the spire of Helpringham gives the illusion of pushing its supporting buttresses outwards, almost to the point of forcing them off the tower. After a mile **turn R** (signed 'Burton Pedwardine'), pass Burton's tiny church on your left, the last standing remains of this shrunken medieval village, then **turn L** (signed 'Scredington') to cross a railway bridge.

In a further 1½ miles you will discover that the next village of Scredington also holds a wealth of historical significance, with evidence of five medieval moated houses, Hall Close being the most extensive and best surviving site. Your route essentially encircles the area of moats. **Turn L** at the first junction (signed 'Northbeck'), and follow a winding lane to a main road (signed 'Scredington'), passing on your right an ancient twin-arched packhorse bridge left high and dry by its modern replacement. **Turn R** (signed 'Scredington') onto the main road and follow it through the village, beyond which you eventually arrive at Mareham Lane, a long straight road of Roman origin.

Turn L onto Mareham Lane (signed 'Threekingham'), immediately **turn R** (signed 'Aswarby'), and continue past two impressive granges on your right until you arrive in the charming stone-built estate village of Aswarby. Decorative cottages and lodges and an equally elaborate family church – with spire of course – accompany you to the main A15. Carefully **turn R** and skirt the parkland, observing a pair of intriguing Georgian columns and a large grassy hummock – reputedly the grave of an elephant who died near here while travelling with a circus in the 19th century. Just past a fine stone hostelry on your left, steeped in hunting tradition and thus named the Tally Ho Inn, **turn L** into a tiny lane (signed 'Aunsby').

Now meander along this lane, through the farming hamlet of Aunsby and past another handsome spire, to the next main road. **Turn R** at the junction (signed 'Sleaford') then **turn L** into another lane (signed 'Aisby'). For 2 miles this road climbs gently away from the lowlands towards a united cluster of hamlets. **Turn L** (signed 'Aisby') to explore the first of these. The lane through Aisby returns you to a wooded road, where you **turn L** at an unsigned T-junction. **Turn R** at the second offshoot (signed 'Oasby') and pass Oasby's Manor House, beneath a large spreading cedar, and the delightfully situated Houblon Arms. Reaching a sign for Heydour, **turn R**. In Heydour you glide by the earthworks of a former Norman castle, a rectory featuring a niched stone carving of a musician said to be an ancient remnant from the castle, and finally the lofty spire of Saint Michael's church – serving the three villages you have just visited (Oasby contributed the inn, while the village green was in Aisby).

Climb out of the wooded dip and **turn L** at a junction (signed 'Culverthorpe'). Culverthorpe is a place of great beauty. On the other side of a tree-fringed lake the parkland rises to the stately classical Hall, dating from the late 17th century. **Turn L** at the farm in Culverthorpe (rather confusingly signposted 'Hall only') and in a few yards **turn R** (signed 'Kelby'). After a roller-coaster mile-and-a-half you arrive at a junction. The least likely option is to your right (signed 'Silk Willoughby – green road only'), but this is your path, and the delightful shaded track soon opens out onto an exhilarating downhill lane which sweeps you all the way to the next main road – the A15. Dismount and cross with care, then go through the gate in front of you to find yourself at the end of a lane leading into Silk Willoughby.

In the heart of this village is the weathered base of an ancient cross bearing carvings of the four Evangelists, as well as the fine tower and parapet of Saint Denys' church soaring gracefully up to the concluding steeple of your journey. Proceed past the church and towards the ever more urban surroundings of Sleaford, with the station finally visible across the tracks in front of you.

SLEAFORD

Sleaford is a cheerful and busy market town built along the twin channels of the River Slea. Some fragments of its 12th century castle remain and the church of Saint Denys in the Market Square is renowned for its flowing window tracery, its monuments to the Carre family and its flawless broach spire reaching to a height of 144 ft. The eight-storey Money's Windmill stands in an open courtyard near to Navigation House and other interesting features around the canal, which enabled goods to be transported easily to and from the mill.

HECKINGTON

Saint Andrew's ranks as one of the country's most complete specimens of Gothic architecture from the Decorated period. Known as the 'Cathedral of the Fens', nowhere are the elaborate window tracery and detailed carving around the Easter Sepulchre bettered. Elsewhere in the village the fully restored windmill is the country's only surviving eight-sailed example, and the Pearoom, a former agricultural sorting warehouse, now houses an art gallery, a craft workshop complex and a tearoom.

16

Boston and the Lincolnshire Coast

15 miles

Boston is a major market town and port whose attractions are too numerous to list here. If you have time to visit only one, do not miss the 365 steps to the top of Saint Botolph's church tower – the Boston 'Stump', from where you can see as far as the distant coast and the Wash beyond. Conversely your level journey across the fens towards this coast and back will be dominated by glorious views of Saint Botolph's. Throughout the ride the exploits of the Pilgrim Fathers are a recurring theme, and there are also a few older tales to tell along the way . . .

Map: OS Landranger 131 Boston & Spalding (GR 327442).

Starting point: The Market Place in central Boston. There is limited parking here, but there are many other well-signed car parks around the town centre. The town is also well served by trains running from several directions.

Refreshments: Boston, of course, lacks nothing in the way of good places to eat and drink. Away from the town you will find inns serving food in the villages of Fishtoft, Butterwick and Freiston.

From Boston Market Place cycle away from the 'Stump' in the direction of South Street, nodding politely to the large statue of Herbert Ingram, the Boston-born founder of the *Illustrated London News*. Pass the Guildhall (once the prison where the Pilgrim Fathers were held) and the handsome Fydell House on your left, and restored maritime buildings lining the riverside opposite. Continue straight on at the traffic lights and, as the deep muddy channel comes alongside, **turn L** into Skirbeck Road (signed 'Fishtoft'). Look for a gravel track on your left leading to the shell of one of Lincolnshire's oldest brick buildings, the three-storey Hussey Tower, dating from 1450 and inspired by Tattershall Castle. Its owner, Lord John Hussey, was executed by Henry VIII in 1537 for failing to deal with the Lincolnshire Rising. The next noteworthy building is the classical frontage of Saint John's on your right, now dwarfed by the metal silos behind. Further on you cross the wide Maud Foster Drain, where the rows of terraces, the narrow streets and the countless public houses indicate the proximity of the docks area, once hugely important.

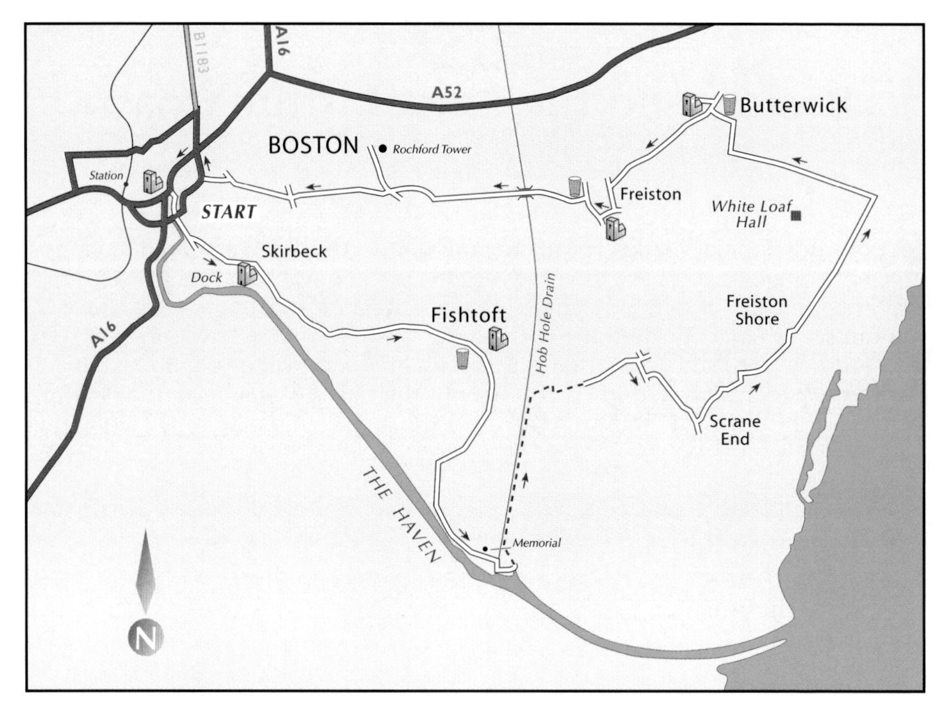

Reaching a church on your right with distinctive porthole windows you realise that you have crossed into the village of Skirbeck, and from here the surroundings become less urban, until eventually open countryside is reached. Stay true to this road until you reach the village of Fishtoft where, unless you wish to visit the large church of Saint Guthlac deep into the village, you **turn R** just past a war memorial into Gaysfield Road (signed 'Pilgrim Fathers Memorial').

When you spot the blue metal rails of a Wesleyan chapel, keep right and follow Scalp Road as it winds towards the raised defences of the ancient sea bank, and finally to its terminus at a picnic site. Here excellent information panels relate the story of the Pilgrim Fathers, the history of the fenlands and the development of the Havenside Country Park. A track around the back of the picnic site leads you to a stone memorial marking the spot from where, in 1607, the first Pilgrim Fathers made their doomed attempt to flee. From here two sea bank paths lead along the shoreline. Select the left-hand bank and cycle along this until you reach the Hobhole Drain, to **turn R** alongside the Drain and, passing the former Jolly Sailor inn on your right, **turn L** (signed 'Lincolnshire Cycle Way') and cross both arms of the Drain. Now **turn L** to follow the surfaced track below the Hobhole Drain until you reach

Nunn's Bridge. Do not cross this bridge but go straight ahead where an untitled lane becomes a permissive cycle track wending a course across open fields.

Go straight ahead where the track rejoins the road and, ⅓ mile later, **turn R** into Cropper's Lane, then immediately **turn L** (signed 'Scrane End'). When you see the immaculate topiary of Miramar House on your right, **turn L** and continue along this narrow lane, going straight over at the crossroads, to reach a T-junction at which you **turn R** towards Freiston Shore. Pass the former Plummer's Hotel and the ruins of the Marine Hotel and **turn R** (signed 'Lincolnshire Cycle Trail') onto a long straight lane between the old Roman sea bank and the new defence.

The nearby building to your left is White Loaf Hall, so named because in Jacobean times the resident monks produced the first ever loaf of white bread here. One gable is surmounted by a loaf-shaped stone bearing the initials 'WLH'. That the monks refined the flour by sieving it through their socks may be pure embellishment!

The lane angles left at a pink cottage and a mile further on you are in the village of Butterwick. **Turn L** at the Five Bells public house and, passing the crooked brick church tower, progress towards the looming tower of Saint James' church in Freiston. As you enter Freiston you will pass a green lane on your right called Foxhole Lane. Locals tell a gruesome story of a man named Fox and a girl, who arranged a meeting here. The girl was first to arrive but, spotting a huge hole newly dug against a tree, she believed that she was about to be murdered and buried by Mr Fox. She hastily climbed high into the tree and hid trembling until he arrived and waited for a time before departing, leaving her free to escape. Otherwise Freiston is an attractive village, built mainly of brick, and the church is the jewel in its crown, all that remains of a substantial 12th century Benedictine priory. Inside the arched Norman doorway hides a curious monument – a 12 ft high font cover intricately carved by a young apprentice. According to legend the master woodworker was so overwhelmed by the beauty of the piece that in a fit of jealous rage he struck the boy dead.

Just past the church **turn R** into Church Road (signed 'Boston'), then **turn L** into Priory Road. In ½ mile you cross a red brick bridge, one of several original bridges spanning the Hobhole Drain, a deep, wide channel 14 miles in length, created in 1812 to drain 40,000 acres of fenland north of Boston. Good views of Saint Botolph's ahead now guide you back towards Boston. At the first roundabout **turn R** into Rochford

Tower Lane and look out for this tower on your right, similar in appearance to the Hussey Tower, dating from the same period and in the same state of decay.

Return to the roundabout and **turn R** into Eastwood Road. Back in Boston **turn L** alongside the Wellington public house and cross the new Vauxhall Bridge over the Maud Foster Drain. At the traffic lights carefully **turn R** onto John Adams Way and immediately **turn L** into Botolph Street. **Turn R** into Pen Street and you soon emerge in Wide Bargate, a large open square in built-up Boston surrounded by more fine buildings. Where this oasis narrows to your left, a short walk through the narrow Strait Bargate will return you to the Market Place from which you began your journey.

SAINT JOHN'S BUILDINGS

Built by Sir George Gilbert Scott in 1837, only the gatehouse and flanking pavilions now remain of this range of classical buildings. Originally the Union Workhouse, Asian families expelled from Uganda by Idi Amin were housed here in the 1970s, and in the Second World War this was the Royal Navy headquarters for the defence of the Wash. It was named HMS *Arbella* after the daughter of the Earl of Lincoln who sailed with the Pilgrim Fathers.

THE PILGRIM FATHERS

In September 1607 a persecuted 'flock' of Puritans, originating from Scrooby in Nottinghamshire, hired a ship to flee from Scotia Creek near Boston to Holland. But the vessel's captain betrayed the fugitives, who were imprisoned in the cells of Boston Guildhall. Later released, they eventually won their passage to Holland a year later, and in 1620 crossed the Atlantic in the Mayflower to found new settlements on America's east coast. In 1630 another wave of Bostonian immigrants founded the town of Boston in Massachusetts, and their preacher John Cotton is commemorated by a memorial and chapel in Saint Botolph's. Scotia Point is the point where the stone memorial, erected in 1957, now stands.

FREISTON SHORE

Attempts in the late 18th century to establish a leading seaside resort here foundered for two reasons. One was the advent of the railways, which meant that people were able to travel more quickly and easily to Skegness, expanding rapidly to the north. Secondly, ever more successful land reclamation methods meant that the sea simply kept moving further and further away. The two hotel buildings you pass still bear witness to the resort's short reign.

17

Grand Mansions and Stately Homes around Grantham

27 miles

Historic stately stone mansions abound in the wooded countryside around Grantham – this adventure takes you on a tour of the finest four, along with their attendant estate villages and churches. In addition, the Roman Ermine Street, the Viking Way and the Great North Road criss-cross the area, and your route links them, embracing a riverside ride through Grantham town centre and an enchanting canal towpath. Other off-road surfaces are encountered, as are several testing gradients, and this should be treated as a full but rewarding day's outing.

Map: OS Landranger 130 Grantham (GR 913359).

Starting point: Four roads lead into Grantham town centre from the A1 – locate the Market Place at the northern end of the High Street, where Watergate and Westgate meet. You may be able to park on the roadside but there is ample signed car parking behind the Market Place. Grantham also offers good rail links from the Newark, Nottingham and Peterborough directions.

Refreshments: Grantham, naturally, offers a full range of refreshment facilities, while superior inns, all serving food, will be found at Woolsthorpe, Denton and Harlaxton. There is a good tearoom within the grounds of Belton House and another at the garden centre on the other side of the A607. In addition, where the A1 is crossed, there is an inn and a garage shop.

Set off from Grantham's Market Place along Westgate, admiring the wonderful variety of shopfronts and houses. Carefully negotiate a busy roundabout (dismount if you prefer) to exit onto the A607 (signed 'Melton Mowbray'), and pass under the railway bridge. Now on Harlaxton Road continue until the A1 has also passed overhead and **turn R** where you see a sign for a cycle path. This track leads through a hawthorn tunnel to the disused Grantham Canal, whose towpath has been restored and resurfaced specifically for cycles. The next 4 miles are a joy. Tall trees stoop to shade the canal, hillsides rising behind them to the woods above. The green surface of the water is rippled by swans and moorhens, and you must tilt your head to clear a succession of elegant low brick bridges, covered

The Riverside Walk and the Witham in Grantham

in ivy. There can be no better way of passing through the English countryside than this.

After two sets of lock gates **turn L** to cross Woolsthorpe Bridge. As you reach the crest of the bridge an apparition appears on the horizon ahead of you, the misty outline of the towers and turrets of Belvoir Castle rising out of the wooded slopes. Pass the Rutland Arms (known locally as 'the Dirty Duck') and **turn L** at the junction. At the crossroads continue ahead to visit the estate village of Woolsthorpe at least as far as the church, before returning to the intersection to **turn R** (signed 'Denton').

Now climb steeply into the woods and cross the Viking Way at Brewer's Grave before swooping into Denton, one of Lincolnshire's best preserved estate villages, a cluster of golden stone buildings of locally quarried ironstone. The grand Perpendicular church tower is the crowning glory here, overlooking one of three lakes and approached via a lane passing the Welby Arms, a stone inn of exquisite appearance and setting. Follow the main road up the hill to the arched gatehouse of Denton Manor and **turn L** (signed 'Harlaxton') to proceed with care along the A607 once more.

In 1½ miles **turn R** into Harlaxton's

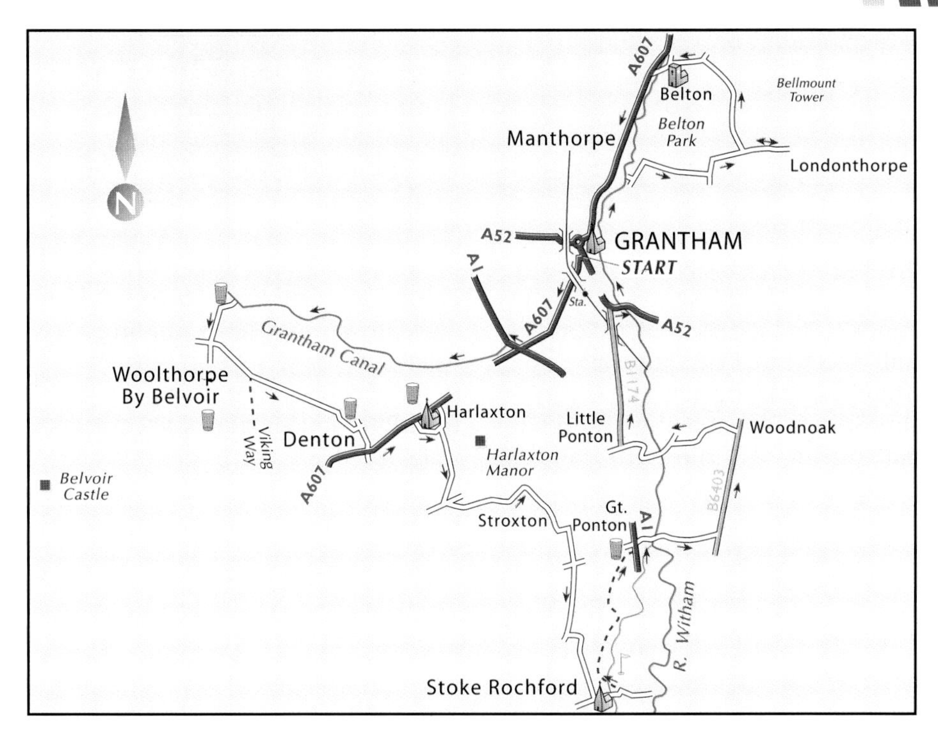

unsigned Rectory Lane, which you follow in a large semi-circle, noting that Harlaxton is also an architectural showcase of stone, brick and timber features. Soon, back at the main road, your gaze is drawn by the colossal stone gateway to your right, and through its railings appears the most breathtaking sight, a distant masterpiece of turrets, gables and chimneys, impossible to take in at once – this fairytale palace is Harlaxton Manor.

Suitably impressed retrace your tracks into Harlaxton but this time **turn L** at the village cross (signed 'Hungerton') and ascend steeply, eventually reaching a T-junction. **Turn L** here (signed 'Grantham'), then immediately **turn R** (signed 'Stroxton') and complete the long gradual descent into the farming hamlet of Stroxton. Passing the duckpond and rounding the bend, **turn R** onto a steep track signposted as 'Gated' and 'Unsuitable for cars'. This neglected lane zigzags towards a crossroads at which you continue straight ahead (signed 'Stoke Rochford'), as far as a lake at the foot of a hill. **Turn L** into Cringle Lane in front of the lake then follow this lovely lane past several farmsteads until it terminates at a junction – here **turn L** into Stoke Rochford. Stoke is another collection of outstanding stone buildings, and the interior of Saint Mary and Saint Andrew's church, containing a wealth of sculpted monuments to the Turnors, should not be missed.

Past the bridge over Cringle Brook **turn L** between high stone walls and onto the driveway leading to Stoke Rochford Hall. The route through this delightful parkland reaches Sir Isaac Newton's obelisk opposite the grand approach to the Hall itself, but you continue straight ahead through an aluminium gate, having absorbed the splendour of the 1840 Hall, created in the style of Harlaxton Manor and now a banqueting and conference centre.

At a sign which declares 'No walkers beyond this point' the route leaves the track and curves to the left, crosses the golf course (please dismount and walk this short stretch), skirts the corner of the wood ahead of you and arrives at a gate in the hedge near to a yellow marker post. Through the gate **turn L** along a short rough field-edge path, **turn R** where this meets a clearer track and, where this track turns to the left, continue instead along a wide grassy 'green lane' directly ahead of you. Congratulating yourself on your excellent path-finding skills, allow this lane to carry you all the way to the Great North Road – the A1.

Cross with the utmost caution (or use the nearby footbridge if preferred) and locate Archer's Way, which directs you into Dallygate in the heart of Great Ponton, below the lofty church tower. Having identified the church's unique weathervane in the shape of a violin, **turn R** here and follow Dallygate over the infant Witham and through a railway bridge to the elevated Ermine Street. **Turn L** along the Roman highway, proceeding as far as a sign for Little Ponton at Woodnook – **turn L** here to descend an unexpected winding valley, steeply banked on each side. At a row of cottages next to a bridleway, **turn R** to wend along Little Ponton's leaf-shaded lane, which returns you to an unsigned crossroads just before the Great North Road. **Turn R** here and head back towards Grantham, where you **turn R** at a set of traffic lights (signed 'A52 Boston') into Bridge End Road.

Where the huge Spitalgate Mill spans the river to your right, **turn L** to follow the cycle-friendly Riverside Walk along the Witham banks, an ingenious way of bypassing Grantham's busy centre. This most enjoyable track continues into the water meadows beyond the formal parks lining Belton Lane, and terminates at a footbridge. Here **turn R** to cross the river and climb back to Belton Lane, onto which you **turn L** and advance to the monumental crested iron gates of Belton House, availing yourself of a short stretch of cycle track. Through the gates admire the mile-distant mansion the way it was intended to be viewed, then continue along Londonthorpe Lane for some distance. Londonthorpe itself is

worth visiting, if only to admire the county's only bus shelter to earn a mention in Pevsner's definitive Buildings of England, a rusticated ex-conduit house with a stone arch surmounted by a carved horse. About turn at the shelter and backtrack for ½ mile to an unsigned turning at Londonthorpe Wood, into which you **turn R**.

Follow this lane through the parklands of Belton House, crossing the avenue sweeping up to the odd tower known as Lord Brownlow's Britches, where the view from the summit over Belton Park is spectacular. **Turn L** at a T-junction and **turn L** again (signed 'Grantham') in Belton village, much of which was laid out by Anthony Salvin in the 1830s – and what a time he had! No two buildings are alike in this village of bizarre stone eccentricities, a suitable hors d'oeuvre for the feast of a visit to glorious Belton House, time hopefully permitting. Past the church and the entrance to the House, **turn L** when you reach the A607 (signed 'Grantham'). This busy road now takes you all the way back into central Grantham, passing through Manthorpe where, if you choose, a footpath conducts you back to the Riverside Walk. Otherwise continue and pass close enough to Saint Wulfram's grand spire to surely justify a tour, and **turn L** at the major junction into Watergate and towards the Market Place once more.

GRANTHAM AND THE CANAL

Who knows what Sir Isaac Newton and Baroness Thatcher might think of their birthplace's famous dismissal as 'the most boring town in England'? In truth the town has a fascinating history, with many sights to interest the visitor. The cathedral-like proportions of Saint Wulfram's church were unrivalled in the 13th century, and beneath the 282 ft high spire – still considered by many to be England's finest – is a unique library of chained books. Long important as a staging post along the Great North Road, Grantham's significance as a trading centre was boosted in 1793 when the 33 miles of canal linking the town with the River Trent in Nottingham were completed. A vigorous restoration programme aims to return the canal, abandoned since 1929, to full working order.

BELVOIR CASTLE

Pronounced 'Beaver', the castle dates from 1800 and is the fourth to be built on this site. The towers and turrets of the exterior are certainly romantic but this castle was never built with defence in mind and inside are rich furnishings and artworks, including a Holbein painting of Henry VIII, since whose reign the Dukes of Rutland have occupied the site. The only conflict the present castle has ever seen is in the shape of today's renowned jousting tournaments, staged regularly in the grounds.

BELTON HOUSE

Built to a design by Sir Christopher Wren and the seat of the Brownlows for 300 years, this paragon of 17th century elegance is perhaps best known for its rich Grinling Gibbons' wood carvings. The church inside the grounds contains an overwhelming display of monuments to the Brownlows and the Custs.

18

Around the Villages of South Kesteven

27 miles

Where the fens end and the rolling hills of Kesteven take over, the countryside is dotted with intriguing stone-built villages, each offering a different excuse to delay you. Two contrasting castles, a single oak of great eminence and a collection of equally distinguished trees are among these. Heading out along the valley of the East Glen River and returning via her westerly twin the route never strays far from the park of noble Grimsthorpe and, though sometimes hilly, remains on firm road surfaces throughout.

Map: OS Landranger 130 Grantham (GR 998250).

Starting point: Corby Glen is just north of the A151 between Bourne and the A1 at Colsterworth. Several roads lead from the A151 into the village, and you should have no trouble parking in or near the Market Square. The nearest railway station is Grantham.

Refreshments: Although no major centres are encountered the area is rich in country inns serving good food, with a fine example to be found in all of the main villages en route.

Head north from Corby Glen's sloping Market Square along High Street, where stone cottages and inns accompany you until the lane bears right past the former Wheatsheaf inn and exits the village. Two miles along this tree-lined lane you come to the most arresting village of Irnham, entirely built in grey stone. Halt at the castellated church gate piers on your right and walk to the churchyard's furthest corner. The church itself is impressive enough, but from here can be sneaked the best views of Irnham Hall's creepered walls and mullioned windows. Built during an era of religious intolerance, the Hall's interior has been discovered to contain a number of 'priest holes' and escape passages. Continuing in your original direction **turn R** opposite the Griffin Inn (signed 'Swinstead') and pass the entrance to the grounds of the Hall. Beyond the spectacle of the stable block's high arch, flanked by colossal octagonal towers, climb out of the village which concludes ½ mile later at an ornate lodge on your right.

At this point **turn L** onto a delightful public bridleway and enjoy views towards the

The duckpond at Castle Bytham

Grimsthorpe estates on your right, possibly startling pheasants and hares on your way. The track – now stony – emerges at a lane onto which you **turn R**, descend to the East Glen River, now bridged but once merely forded. Now rise into the hamlet of Bulby, **turn R** at the junction (signed 'Elsthorpe') and follow an undulating lane above the East Glen valley. Elsthorpe is little more than a collection of farmsteads and, from here, the lane soon passes over the East Glen and approaches Grimsthorpe, the elegant castle parapets now looming ahead of you.

Reaching the busier A151, the village of Grimsthorpe and the excellent Black Horse Inn lie to the right, but to continue on your route **turn L** (signed 'Bourne') and, keeping the castle grounds to your right, wend your way towards Edenham. Here the church of Saint Michael guards an astounding display of monuments to the Willoughbys and Berties of Grimsthorpe Castle. In addition the memorials of the Heathcotes, another notable local family, were moved here from Normanton when the church there became threatened by the creation of nearby Rutland Water. The vicarage next to the church is said to be where Charles Kingsley wrote *Hereward the Wake*.

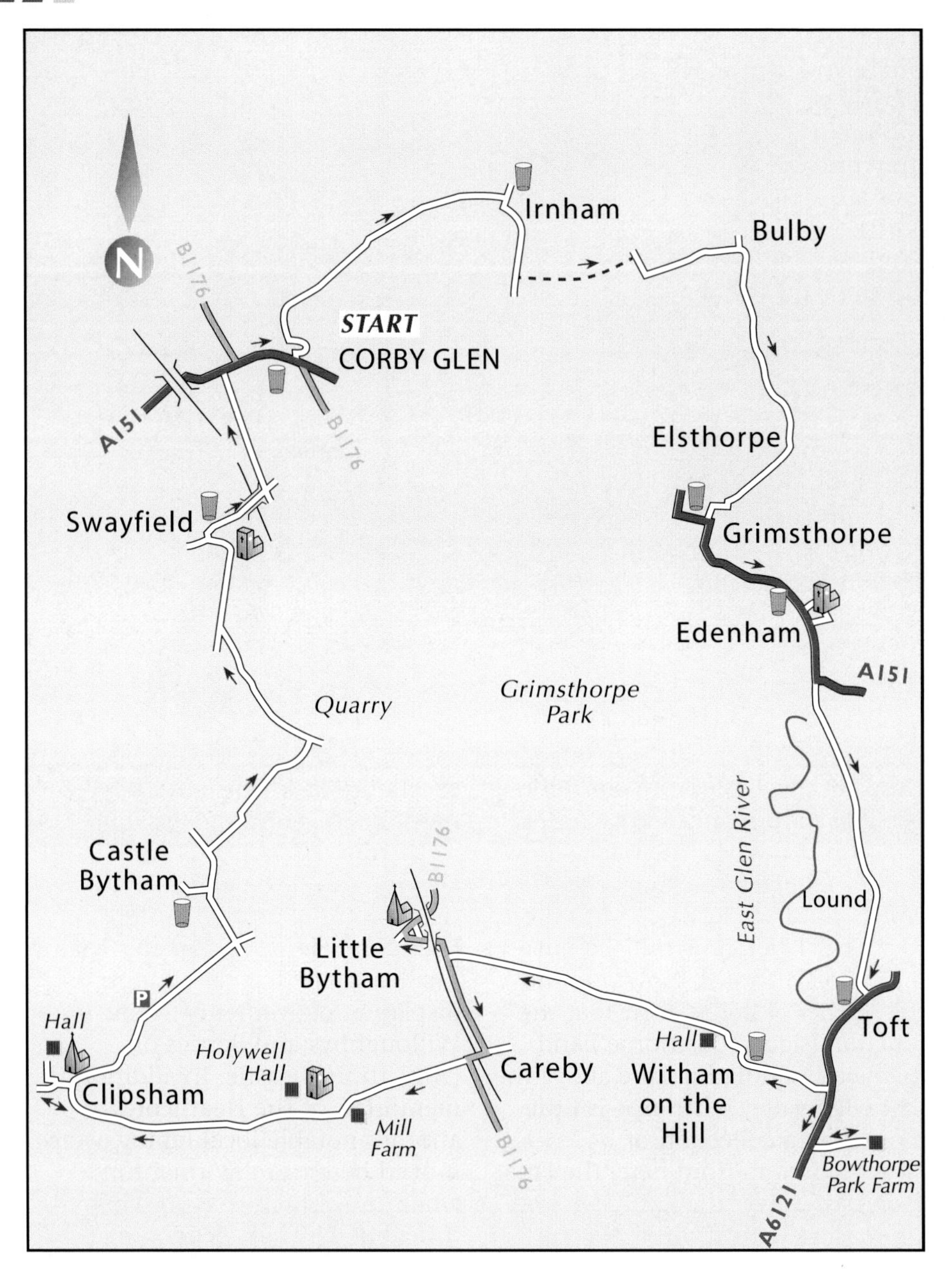

Half a mile through Edenham, where the main road bends left, **turn R** (signed 'Lound') and proceed along this tranquil little lane for a good 2 miles until it turns sharply and ends abruptly at the Toft House Hotel. Here **turn R** (signed 'Stamford') onto the A6121

which soon arrives at a crossroads where you should **turn R** again (clearly signed 'Witham-on-the-Hill'). But first you may wish to stray past the crossroads until you spot a sign on your left for the Bowthorpe Oak, one of the wonders of Lincolnshire. Here a pleasant track guides you to Bowthorpe Park Farm and the tree whose 40 ft girth is England's largest, earning it a place in the *Guinness Book of Records*.

Now back on the road into Witham-on-the-Hill pass the Six Bells inn and descend to the green where stand the ancient village stocks beneath their unusual circular tiled canopy. Continuing past Witham Hall look left to admire a succession of pillared stone arches and progress for a full 2 miles before you **turn R** into Little Bytham at the T-junction (signed 'Castle Bytham'). This village is dominated by the colossal arches of the Great Northern Railway but manages to retain its charm. **Turn L** into a narrow lane before the ford and cross a footbridge to enter Church Lane which, not surprisingly, leads you up to Saint Medard's. Here **turn R** and, just before a stone inn renamed the Mallard in celebration of that train's record steam speed of 126 mph here in 1938, **turn R** again.

Pass the ford once more and progress to Careby where a sharp bend takes you over the railway bridge. Beyond the bridge continue straight ahead (signed 'Holywell'), where two regal avenues of horse chestnut trees inside the adjacent fields indicate your route to Holywell. Here, opposite Mill Farm, a large lake is beautifully set in wooded parkland leading to the stone basin of the well itself next to Holywell Hall and the private church. **Turn L** at the first junction (signed 'Stamford'), **turn R** at the next (signed 'Pickworth') and continue along the southern edge of the park, peering carefully for glimpses of the cluster of buildings below.

Another lengthy but charming lane now follows the valley up to Clipsham, where the mellow stone buildings are crowned by the church steeple. The churchyard below is lined with trimmed yew arbours – a taste of what is in store! From the church return to the main T-junction, **turn L** (signed 'Castle Bytham') and follow the edge of the wood until you are suddenly greeted by an amazing sight. From a small lodge to your left a wide avenue stretches towards the opulence of Clipsham Hall, and lining this drive are 150 mature yew trees, each immaculately cropped and with varied designs clipped into the topiary, including an elephant, the three bears and even the first moon landing.

A mile past here **turn L** at a major crossroads (signed 'Swayfield') and enter Castle Bytham, a village well worth a detailed exploration. Two inns and the village shop can be found in the maze of steep, narrow streets to the left, while on the right rise the grassy ramparts of the former fortifications. Passing a quaint duckpond leave Castle Bytham and **turn R** where you see a sign for Counthorpe. Counthorpe Lane is steep at first but later plummets towards the entrance to a large limestone quarry. **Turn L** here (signed 'Swayfield'), carefully locating your lane below the quarry fence. This idyllic wooded lane climbs along the valley contours to eventually emerge at an unsigned T-junction – **turn R** here to enter Swayfield, a mainly farming community and the final village of your excursion.

Turn R (signed 'Swinstead') into Swayfield High Street, pass the Royal Oak and the beacon at the entrance to the church driveway, and veer to the right to leave the village. **Turn L** (signed 'Corby Glen') beyond the railway bridge and, a mile later, **turn R** (also signed 'Corby Glen') onto the A151. Station Road now leads you over the West Glen River and once more into the peaceful village of Corby Glen, and your starting place in the Market Square.

CORBY GLEN

Only in 1955 did Corby receive its 'Glen' to distinguish it from the town in Northamptonshire. Each October this village's former market tradition is revived for the Sheep Fair, held since 1238, and in the churchyard the headstone of Joe Wright, one of the auctioneers at the Fair, bears a famous epitaph:

> At last old death with visage queer
> Assumed Joe's trade of auctioneer
> Made him the lot to practise on
> With going going and anon
> He knocked him down. So poor Joe's gone.

GRIMSTHORPE CASTLE AND CASTLE BYTHAM

The historic castles of these two villages could not be more dissimilar. Castle Bytham was established soon after the Norman Conquest. It is certain that sturdy stone walls rose from these steep moated earthworks in medieval times, but today not a stone remains and Bytham's history is shrouded in mystery. Grimsthorpe, on the other hand, developed from a medieval tower into a 16th century Tudor mansion. When the illustrious Sir John Vanbrugh added the dramatic baroque north front, Grimsthorpe assumed the mantle of Lincolnshire's grandest country house. Well stocked with fine paintings and furniture inside, the castle grounds are bounded by a 16 mile perimeter wall and were, of course, laid out by Lancelot 'Capability' Brown.

CLIPSHAM YEW TREE AVENUE

Amos Alexander, head forester at Clipsham in 1870, lived in the lodge and took up the hobby of creating figures by clipping the yew trees outside his house. This so impressed the squire that Amos was given the task of cutting figures and scenes into every yew in the avenue. By 1955 years of neglect had left the avenue overgrown, but the Forestry Commission introduced a topiary training scheme, following which the Yew Tree Avenue was restored to its original standard.

19
From Holbeach to the Wash

25 miles

You might find that the Lincolnshire Fens are an acquired taste. This is a land of moods and atmospheres, more intense at dawn and dusk, when a wealth of colourful views extend across vast, endless skies. Historic market towns and galleon-like churches illuminate your journey around an area which has been fighting the battle for land against the sea since Roman times. You will also encounter a pair of inland lighthouses and the story of a king who lost the Crown Jewels. It's all on excellent road surfaces – and not a hill to be seen all day!

Map: OS Landranger 131 Boston & Spalding (GR 358248).

Starting point: The town of Holbeach sits one mile south of the A17, midway between Sleaford and King's Lynn. Three well-signed roads lead from the A17 into the centre of Holbeach, where you should seek out one of several small car parks. Sadly the rail network no longer serves this area.

Refreshments: All types of refreshment are on offer in Holbeach, and you will find many good inns along the route – the Chequers in Gedney Dyke being of particular note. Fleet Hargate, as well as its public houses, can boast two teashops. There are no inns, however, between Sutton Bridge and Lutton.

From the mighty spire of All Saints' church set off east along Holbeach High Street, flanked by tall prosperous-looking buildings of many styles. In less than a mile, now in more residential surroundings, you **turn R** at a petrol station into Branch's Lane, startled by the fact that you are at once in open countryside. **Turn L** when you spot Hazelwood Lane which twists and turns until its junction with Hocklesgate – here **turn R** into the small village of Fleet.

Pass a delightful thatched lychgate leading to the stately spire of Saint Mary Magdalen, whose tower is divorced from the main body of the church, and **turn L** into Eastgate. Past the brick range of the former railway station Fleet becomes Fleet Hargate, into whose main street you **turn R**, opposite the trim cream and green woodwork of Fleet House. Stay true to this road which evolves into Top's Gate beyond Chestnut Farm and Teashop, and changes again into Church End as you enjoy exceptional views of Gedney's

The River Nene at Sutton Bridge

breathtaking church. Twin ranks of huge clear windows make the church seem almost transparent, but the tower, whose steeple was planned but never built, has had to make do with its much-derided 'little lead spike'. Reaching Linden House, where the herringbone brickwork dates from 1720, cross the busy A17 with great care. Cut through to the Old Black Lion ahead of you and, facing this inn's black and gold Edwardian façade, **turn R** to wind between Chapelgate's interesting buildings leading you to a large new roundabout.

Turn L onto the B1359 (signed 'Long Sutton') and proceed towards the town of that name. The A17 now bypasses the town thus robbing it of much passing trade, and an air of neglect hangs over the nonetheless handsome Georgian houses along the Main Street. And nestling in a corner of the Market Place the magnificence of Saint Mary's church is undeniable. Like Fleet, its tower was originally set apart from the nave, and it still boasts the country's best preserved lead spire. Continue straight ahead through Long Sutton – unless you intend to visit the Butterfly and Wildlife Park, where inmates range from tarantulas to wallabies.
Three long straight miles further on you find yourself in the rather

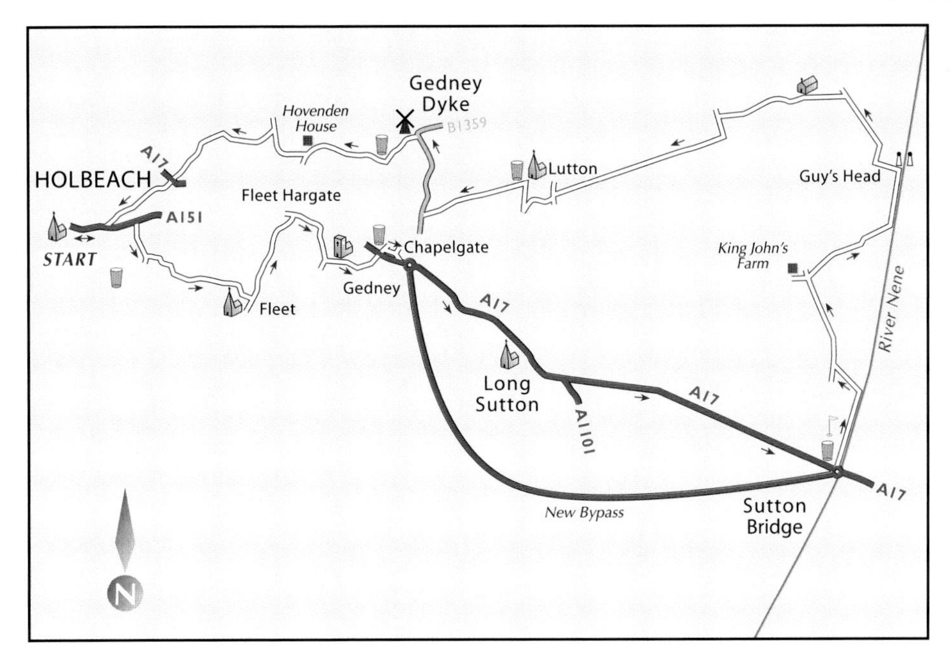

industrial community of Sutton Bridge. Here, having inspected the huge hydraulic swing bridge rising from a tangle of crumbling wooden quays, you **turn L** at the Bridge Hotel to follow the course of the River Nene. This road leads you past old dockside buildings and modern cranes offloading timber and steel before veering quite suddenly over a cattle-grid and onto an entirely rural chestnut-lined lane. **Turn R** at the unsigned T-junction and, a mile later, **turn R** again at King John's Farm (signed 'Gedney Drove End'). Another mile leads you back to the banks of the Nene, which you follow as far as a curious white lighthouse at Guy's Head, almost hidden in the trees. Its twin is more clearly visible on the opposite bank of the wide muddy river.

The lane now leads inland along the course of the former sea wall. Passing a wayside chapel you continue along this open lane for an enjoyable 4 miles to eventually **turn L** at its terminus (signed 'Long Sutton'). Almost immediately you **turn R** into Colley's Gate, **turn R** again into Pudding Poke Lane and, at a cairn commemorating the Silver Jubilee of 1977, **turn R** once more. Now in Lutton **turn L** into Roper's Gate (signed, 'Gedney Dyke') where an inn called the Jolly Crispin faces Lutton's delightful stone church steeple atop its brick tower. **Turn R** at the next T-junction (signed 'Gedney Dyke') and, where Engine Dyke meets Main Street in Gedney Dyke, **turn L** (signed 'Holbeach Hurn').

Past the distinctive Chequers inn and restaurant your lane guides you towards the landscaped grounds of Hovenden House, now a Cheshire Home and just visible between stately stone gate piers topped with urns. **Turn R** at a sign for Holbeach Hurn to continue the circuit of this veritable arboretum. Ignore a turn to the left, pass a small private golf course on your right, and only then **turn L** into Hurn Road (signed 'Holbeach'). Hurn Road wends its way back to the busy A17, where you cross carefully and **turn R** for a few yards in the direction of Sleaford. Now **turn L** into Foxes Low Road which leads you back towards Fleet Road – here **turn R** (signed 'Holbeach') and retrace your journey's opening half-mile into the splendid surroundings of Holbeach, back to the church in the town centre.

HOLBEACH

Bisected by the Greenwich Meridian, Holbeach is an ancient market town, though its cornmarket and horse fairs have now vanished. The word 'beach' indicates that the coastline was once just 2 miles away, and, as the seas have receded, the parish has grown to become England's largest. The spire of All Saints' church can only claim to be the country's fifth tallest, but this is still a showcase of late Decorated Gothic building, dominating the centre of the town and set against a backdrop of tall larch and ash trees. The unusual twin turrets of the entrance porch are said to be from nearby Moulton Castle.

SUTTON BRIDGE

The town only came into existence in 1831 when Telford and Rennie threw a wooden bridge over the River Nene at this point. Replaced first by Robert Stephenson's swing bridge 20 years later, the bridge was again renewed at the end of the 19th century to serve both rail and road traffic. The golf course you pass near the modern quayside hides the tale of Sutton Bridge's failed ambition as a major port. This site was opened as a splendid new dock in 1881. However, the same year the shifting sands beneath the foundations led to the collapse of the dock walls and the abandonment of the entire project.

KING JOHN'S TREASURE

King John's Farm is on the site of the house where the treacherous King John rested on his way from King's Lynn to Spalding in 1216. While he took the longer but safer inland route his baggage train of wagons and packhorses was ordered to attempt the shortest route across the estuary marshland, a journey only possible at low water. But the convoy (including the King's valuable treasures) was overtaken by the swiftly incoming tide and swept away into the Wash. Although the King escaped this disaster his treasure was never located, and only a week later he died of fever at Newark Castle.

GUY'S HEAD LIGHTHOUSES

These twin 'lighthouses' were erected on either side of the River Nene in 1826 to commemorate the completion of a river improvement scheme. In the 19th century the lighthouse on the west bank served as a Customs and Excise station, while the east lighthouse is best known as the home of Sir Peter Scott, celebrated naturalist and painter, to whom a 10 mile coastal walk from this point is dedicated.

20
Crowland and the Deepings

26 miles

This route takes the form of a figure-of-eight, permitting an additional choice of two shorter rides if preferred. The first half is a fenland outing along the banks of the River Welland to the atmospheric ruins of a medieval abbey, the second is an excursion through more lush surroundings, and a series of striking villages dotted around a watery landscape of streams, bridges, mills and meadows. A stone-built market town, hidden country inns, and a quirky display of stone carvings make this a fascinating route throughout, and it is entirely across level terrain and on sound road surfaces.

Map: OS Landranger 142 Peterborough (GR 138099).

Starting point: The Market Place in Market Deeping, where the A15 and the A16 cross. If you cannot park in the Market Place there is a large car park next to the shopping area behind the Bull.

Refreshments: Several excellent inns serve food and drink along the way (in particular in the villages of Frognall, West Deeping, Greatford, Baston and Langtoft), and you will find a wide range of refreshment places in the Deepings and Crowland.

From the centre of Market Deeping, near to the stone bridge over the Welland, advance east through the narrowing Market Place. After a short distance go straight on at a roundabout, then **turn R** at a major junction (signed 'Crowland'), enjoying glimpses of the River Welland running behind the houses to your right. Passing the three reflected arches of the Deeping Gate bridge, the road then wends towards Deeping Saint James, flanked by fine stone houses punctuated by several public houses. Beyond the ancient steps of the village cross you reach another junction. Do not follow the sign for Crowland but continue along the Welland bank into Eastgate.

Soon this road skews away from the river to a tall, neat signal box at another junction. **Turn R** (signed 'Crowland'), cross the tracks, and continue past a succession of lakes towards the Welland once more. Follow the road left upon reaching the river bank. At first the levee screens the river but after a mile the route ascends this bank, and from here a thrilling view is unveiled. To your left these vast 'deepings', England's most fertile

The millpond behind Maxey Mill

land, stretch into the distance while to the right the wide Welland leads your gaze to the vague grey outline of the ruined abbey in Crowland.

Simply follow this riverside lane for 3 miles as far as a tall white octagonal water tower, at which you **turn R** (signed 'Crowland') over Fen Bridge. The next ½ mile is actually a causeway over the washland – note the raised plankways on your left, although modern drainage methods make this area unlikely to flood again. As you rise onto the high banks built to protect Crowland from the high waters of the Welland, **turn L** at the T-junction (signed 'Crowland'). Around a shallow bend **turn R** (signed 'Peterborough') into North Street, which leads you into the centre of Crowland. From the unique Trinity Bridge the abbey is along East Street to your left, but Crowland warrants an extensive exploration.

The next section could not be more simple, and you retrace your tracks for 4½ miles, as far as the junction at the brick signal box, where you **turn R** (signed 'Deeping Saint James'). Beyond a crossroads Custom Road bends left to become Hard's Lane, from which you **turn L** onto a lesser lane (signed 'Frognall'). Follow this twisting lane all the way to Spalding Road,

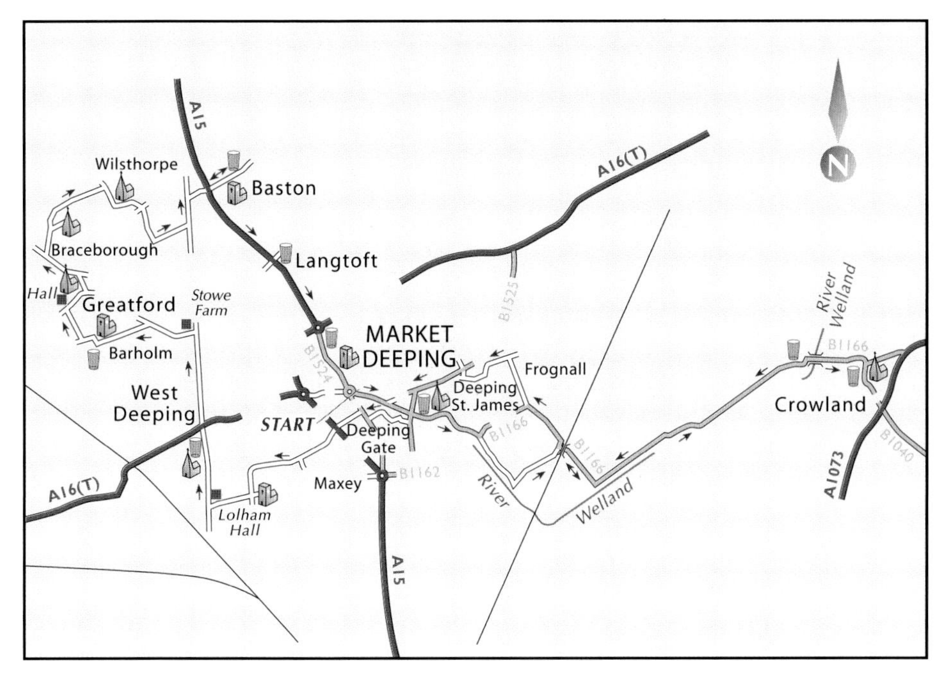

into which you **turn L** (signed 'Market Deeping'), to re-enter the built-up area of the Deepings. Immediately past a large school on the left, **turn L** and continue unerringly ahead, along Park Road, into Bell Lane, past the Bell where this track brings you back to the Welland, and even straight over the stone bridge on the other side of the road in front of you.

Over the bridge **turn R** into Sutton's Lane, which twists left and right until it reaches Lincoln Road. **Turn R** (signed 'Market Deeping'), making use of this short stretch of cycle lane, then **turn L** when you see a barred gate and a 'Public Bridleway' sign opposite Maxey House. This is Mill Lane, which leads you into Maxey, carefully crossing the busy bypass via two more barred gates on the way. The grand old stone houses and thatches of Maxey will repeat themselves as you travel from village to village. Beyond a splendid old corn mill built in 1779, you reach a crossroads at a church. **Turn R** here (signed 'West Deeping'), and then **turn R** again (also signed 'West Deeping') at the Lolham Hall junction. You are now on the old Roman King Street, a branch of Ermine Street.

West Deeping offers good views towards Saint Andrew's church and the nearby watermill, and through the village you continue straight ahead over the A16. A mile into this landscape of lakes, converted for recreational use from former sand and gravel pits, **turn L** (signed 'Barholm'), and approach the village of that name. In the heart of Barholm you should investigate a lane to the left as far as a hidden public house and the Old Hall, before continuing along your original route. Soon spotting a sign for Greatford you **turn R**, and **turn R** again at the next T-junction to approach this enchanting village. Everything in Greatford exudes charm, from the walled grounds of the Hall and the church's wonderful broach spire to the handsome village inn – and those sculptures!

Turn L at the village's main junction (signed 'Braceborough') and in another ½ mile **turn R** (also signed 'Braceborough'). Braceborough is an old spa village, and, beyond the village, the route crosses the East Glen River before reaching another T-junction, at which you **turn R** (signed 'Greatford') into the village of Wilsthorpe. Pass through Wilsthorpe and cross a series of white-railed bridges before you **turn L** at one junction, then **turn L** again at another (both signed 'Baston'). At another sign for Baston **turn R** into Greatford Road and the village of Baston itself, whose Main Street on the other side of the main A15 is well worth exploring as far as the Baskerville Arms.

Return to the A15 and **turn L** onto it (signed 'Deeping'). Proceed with care to the next stone village, Langtoft, like Baston strung out between King Street and its Roman fellow, the Car Dyke waterway. From the tall graceful spire of the church in Langtoft, continue south along Peterborough Road, negotiating a busy roundabout where you meet the Deeping bypass, before Church Street brings you back to the Market Place in the heart of Market Deeping.

CROWLAND

Croyland Abbey in Crowland was founded by Saint Guthlac, a 7th century fenland hermit, on what was then an island surrounded by marshland. Prior to the Dissolution it had become Lincolnshire's largest monastery, and the tower, the west front and the remains of the nave are still spectacular today. The town's unique Trinity Bridge dates from the 14th century, its three arches spanning the three streams which then flowed down the middle of the wide streets to meet here. Look up from here to spot a thatched cup and saucer built into the roof of the teashop.

GREATFORD

As well as its obvious charms Greatford boasts a unique legacy, a wealth of sculptured stone curiosities carved by Major Fitzwilliam, owner of Greatford Hall, in the 1930s. Dotted around the village centre you will come across giant coronets, mushrooms, obelisks and an elephant, to name but a few.